RELLIS RECOLLECTIONS

Number 131

Centennial Series of the Association of Former Students,
Texas A&M University

For three-quarters of a century the site of today's RELLIS Campus has seen history made in many ways. Courtesy of (*clockwise from top left*): Cushing Memorial Library & Archives, Texas A&M University; US Air Force; Cushing Memorial Library & Archives; and Texas A&M Transportation Institute.

RELLIS RECOLLECTIONS

75 Years of Learning, Leadership, and Discovery

Tim Gregg

TEXAS A&M UNIVERSITY PRESS   COLLEGE STATION

First edition

This paper meets the requirements of ANSI/NISO Z39.48-1992 (Permanence of Paper).
Binding materials have been chosen for durability.
Manufactured in the United States of America

Library of Congress Cataloging-in-Publication Data

Names: Gregg, Tim, author. | Sharp, John (John Spencer), writer of foreword.
Title: RELLIS recollections : 75 years of learning, leadership, and discovery / Tim Gregg.
Other titles: Centennial series of the Association of Former Students, Texas A&M University ; no. 131.
Description: First edition. | College Station : Texas A&M University Press, [2019] | Series: Centennial series of the Association of Former Students, Texas A&M University ; number 131 | Includes index.
Identifiers: LCCN 2019021687 | ISBN 9781623498474 (cloth) | ISBN 9781623498481 (ebook)
Subjects: LCSH: Texas A & M University System. RELLIS Campus—Biography. | Texas A & M University System. Riverside Campus—Biography. | Texas A & M University System—Alumni and alumnae—Biography. | Agricultural and Mechanical College of Texas—Alumni and alumnae—Biography. | College campuses—Texas—Bryan—History. | Bryan Air Force Base (Tex.)—Biography. | Bryan Army Air Field (Tex.)—Biography.
Classification: LCC LD5309 .G74 2019 | DDC 378.764/242—dc23
LC record available at https://lccn.loc.gov/2019021687

See www.rellisrecollections.org

This book is dedicated to Wally Moon: honored Aggie, baseball great, and best man to my wife and me. It is from the telling of his story that my understanding of the extraordinary history of today's RELLIS Campus took hold

Courtesy of Cushing Memorial Library & Archives, Texas A&M University.

CONTENTS

Courtesy of the Texas A&M University System.

FOREWORD
RELLIS Recollections

When I first conceived the idea of the RELLIS Campus, it was to create a research magnet to attract government and corporate partners as well as an academic alternative for students who want to live in Bryan-College Station but who—for whatever reason—do not attend Texas A&M University.

I thought it was time that The Texas A&M University System better utilized the 2,000-acre tract that had played such a pivotal role in World War II and the Korean conflict as well as the Bryan-College Station economy at one time.

Frankly, despite the best of intentions, the site's potential had never been realized after its military operations shut down and the air base's storied structures began to fall into disrepair.

Against that backdrop, I announced on May 1, 2016, a four-year, $350 million construction plan—with more to come. But sometimes in our rush to embrace the future, we pave over our past. As a history buff, I didn't want to do that. That's why I asked author Tim Gregg to begin researching the history of the site that is today the RELLIS Campus.

You are holding the result of his hard work. In *RELLIS Recollections: 75 Years of Learning, Leadership, and Discovery*, Tim has captured both the monumental challenges of a nation at war as well as the more mundane moments of everyday life from that time to today.

Take the book's cover photograph for instance. It's a scene from June 6, 1943, and the dedication of Bryan Army Air Field. Thousands came out that day to honor America and pay tribute to the men and women who would serve our nation from the banks of the Brazos River.

In this book, and on the companion website at www.rellisrecollections.org, Tim has put together dozens of stories about people who played a key role in creating the RELLIS legacy. Among them: banker Travis B. Bryan, the godfather of Bryan Field; aviation pioneer Col. Joseph Duckworth, history's first "hurricane hunter; and astronaut Buzz Aldrin, who nearly died as a student pilot at Bryan Air Force Base before his successful walk on the moon.

Thanks to the cooperation of so many, Tim has captured in this book, and in several dozen oral histories, the stories about everyone from Travis B. Bryan, the godfather of Bryan Army Air Field; to

Colonel Joseph Duckworth and his historic flight into a hurricane; to astronaut Buzz Aldrin, whose recollections include a near-fatal crash while a student pilot at Bryan Air Force Base.

Tim also tracked the postwar years, telling the story of how Texas A&M University came into possession of the closed air base and the many research, training, and testing efforts at what was most recently called the Riverside Campus until 2016.

Working with the Texas Historical Commission, the Texas A&M System is also seeking to preserve historic structures at the RELLIS site and commemorating ones that couldn't be saved. This book, and the oral histories that can be found at rellisrecollections.org, are a part of our salute to the past as we look to the future of the RELLIS Campus.

Someday, I predict there will be tens of thousands of students pursuing their education on one side of the RELLIS Campus, while on the other side our System's best researchers will be working alongside partners from the military, government agencies, and the private sector to build a better tomorrow. The fact that the US Army is returning to the site of the old Bryan Army Air Field as the Army Futures Command adds a certain symmetry to the RELLIS story.

May they take their inspiration from the stories you will find here.

John Sharp
Chancellor
The Texas A&M University System

PREFACE

My introduction to what today is called the RELLIS Campus came in 2010 as I sought to tell the story of the best Texas Aggie I'll ever know.

Wally Moon played baseball and basketball at the A&M College of Texas in the years after World War II. As a Major League Baseball player, he earned National League Rookie of the Year honors with the St. Louis Cardinals in 1954.

Wally then won three World Series championships as a member of the Los Angeles Dodgers, the last of which came in 1965, his final year in the big leagues.

Wally's life was a counterpoint to a well-known baseball adage: Nice guys *don't always* finish last.

Nearly a decade ago, I collaborated with Wally to write his memoir: *Moon Shots: Reflections on a Baseball Life.* I put a few thousand miles on my car to do so. While Wally enjoyed retirement with his wife Bettye in Bryan, Texas, I lived and worked as a marketing and communications consultant in the Houston area.

We frequently met in his home to discuss his story and review our work.

Contained within the 340 pages of the finished book was a single paragraph about the "old Bryan Air Force Base," the location upon which the RELLIS Campus has now emerged.

Thus, while I was by no means an expert on the subject, at least I had a small point of reference from which to attempt to build a RELLIS history.

So for me, that history and this book begin with a tribute to my good friend.

Wally Moon grew up in the tiny Arkansas community of Bay. He arrived at Texas A&M in the late summer of 1947, a letter of admittance to the school in hand. Wally had never seen the A&M campus, nor met his future coach—in both baseball and basketball—Marty Karow.

At that point, Wally also wasn't completely certain as to what an "Aggie" actually was.

Athletic recruiting was much different in those days.

Upon stepping off the bus, Wally found the A&M campus nearly deserted. Not until he ventured into a bookstore did he discover that the vast majority of incoming freshmen were not going to be on campus.

They were located at a place called "The Annex."

Wally also learned that day that all freshmen, including himself, were going to be known as "fish" during their first year at A&M.

In *Moon Shots*—and on Wally's behalf—I wrote:

"The Annex was the old Bryan Air Force Base which had been converted into student housing to accommodate the sizable influx of war veterans who were taking advantage of the Servicemen's Readjustment Act, more commonly called the 'GI Bill.' My freshman class of 1947 included more than 1,500 newly enrolled veterans."

Eight years later, in researching this history of the old Bryan Air Force Base, I discovered a couple errors in my *Moon Shots* reference to the place.

While there were "newly enrolled" veterans housed at The Annex, the majority of those 1,500 souls living on the site of the deactivated Bryan Army Air Field—it wouldn't become known as "Bryan Air Force Base" until the instillation was again opened at the outset of the Korean War in 1951—were Wally's age and from his socioeconomic circumstance: farm and small-town boys in pursuit of a college education.

And as I've learned, Aggies aren't known by the year they arrive on campus but by the year they are expected to graduate.

Unlike most of his fellow members of the Class of '51, Wally was spared The Annex experience. Freshmen athletes in those postwar years lived in Hart Hall, the A&M athletic dormitory of the day.

Wally did visit The Annex once during his fish year. He told me the experience left him "depressed."

Wally's story, in his own words, is now contained on the "RELLIS Recollections" website, which serves as a companion to this book. Both works seek to chronicle the legacy upon which the RELLIS Campus has been built.

Within the confines of this project can be found scores of stories from dozens of people with direct experience or first-hand knowledge of the history of what is now RELLIS.

Some of those people I met thanks to Wally Moon.

Wally Moon served as best man at my wedding, and when my wife, Nancy, took a job as a professor within the Texas A&M College of Engineering, she and I relocated from Houston to the College Station area in the summer of 2017.

Thanks to that move, I got to spend a lot more time with Wally. In doing so, I became aware that he was slowing down significantly in the ninth decade of his life. Once a week, I'd drop by the one-bedroom apartment in the Bryan retirement community where he lived after Bettye's death to check in on him and spend time talking . . . about a variety of subjects.

His door was rarely locked and, usually, I found him resting in his recliner.

"I almost fell asleep waiting for you," he would often say.

When I told Wally I had been hired by the Texas A&M University System to put together a history of the old Bryan Air Force Base, he suggested that I meet some of the cadets who had lived there.

"And where would I do that?" I asked.

"At the old Briarcrest Country Club," he replied. Through Wally, I learned that on the first Tuesday of every month, members of the A&M Classes of '50, '51, and '52 get together for lunch at what had become the Phillips Events Center after ownership of the property passed to the City of Bryan.

"A lot of those guys lived at The Annex," he said.

"Well, when I do pay them a visit, would you like to join me?" I asked my friend.

"Indeed, I would."

A few months later, on February 6, 2018, Wally and I made the five-minute drive from his retirement home to his former golfing grounds. By then, Wally wasn't getting out much. In the car he admitted it had been some time since he'd dined with his friends.

"I hope they remember me," he laughed.

Wally was always a sharply dressed man. That day, he looked particularly dapper, sporting a maroon blazer over an even darker maroon polo shirt. His khaki pants were neatly creased and not a single hair on his head was out of place.

I do believe he may have even trimmed his famous "unibrow" for the occasion.

As we entered the downstairs meeting room where the monthly gathering took place, Wally was instantly and enthusiastically hailed by those in attendance.

Making the rounds, he introduced me to each of his friends. I explained that my presence was at the behest of Chancellor John Sharp who, in appreciation for the group's anticipated involvement in the RELLIS history project, would be picking up the tab for everyone's food and drink.

The group—about two dozen octogenarians—was a lively bunch. They told stories on one another, reminisced about past glories, and tried to recall "whatever happened" to this or that person who had lived at The Annex with them.

Wally had a terrific time.

Afterwards, on our way back to his apartment, Wally expressed gratitude for my role in getting him back together with his pals.

"Just a part of my job," I said. "Literally. Today was a part of my job."

He laughed and sat quietly for a time. Then he offered a not-unexpected view on life from what he and I had started to call "the late innings."

"It's a good thing we can get together like this," he said, 'You know, there's a pretty good chance not all of us will be around the next time."

Unexpectedly, Wally died three days later.

In March, I returned to the old Briarcrest Club to pay tribute to Wally Moon with his friends. While there, I interviewed several of the attendees about time spent and experiences had at The Annex.

So you see, a bit of Wally Moon lives on in these pages, and I dedicate this book to him.

Wally was pleased the RELLIS project would give me a chance to write again. We both loved the experience of telling his remarkable life story. Wally also thought the RELLIS project would help me "get acquainted around town." And, in that respect, he was absolutely right.

It has been a privilege to collect stories from so many kind and interesting people. And, the story will continue. With the publication of this book, my hope is that more people will come forth wanting to share their own recollections about RELLIS.

Wally told me once, "You can't spell "history" without a "s-t-o-r-y."

To add your RELLIS story, simply go to the website, rellisrecollections.org, and drop me a line.

Both the website and this book seek to showcase a remarkable legacy of not just a place but also those who sought to find their better selves there.

That legacy lives on, now revitalized and continues a unique and proud tradition, one which embodies Respect, Excellence, Loyalty, Leadership, Integrity, and Selfless Service, the core values of Texas A&M:

RELLIS.

The author and his wife, Nancy Currie-Gregg, with Wally Moon at a Texas A&M Athletic Hall of Fame banquet at Kyle Field. Photo by author.

Young Texas Aggie Wally Moon. Courtesy of Texxas A&M Athletics.

Courtesy of Cushing Memorial Library & Archives, Texas A&M University.

RELLIS RECOLLECTIONS

www.rellisrecollections.org

The flight control tower on today's RELLIS Campus dates back to the 1950s Korean War era of Bryan Air Force Base. Photo by author.

INTRODUCTION
One Place. Many Names

Providing a balanced and documented telling of the RELLIS Campus history is a curious challenge, in large part because a lack of "permanence" permeates the location's past.

Simply put, the one place has been known by many names.

- Community of Riverside
- Bryan Army Air Field
- The Annex (of the A&M College of Texas)
- "Lower Slobovia" (popularized by cartoonist Al Capp in the comic strip *L'il Abner*, and a term, according to Wikipedia, used to describe "a place which is underdeveloped, socially backward, remote, impoverished or unenlightened")
- Bryan Air Force Base
- "Hell in Texas" or any of a number of mostly unprintable *sobriquets* used by Bryan Air Force Base enlisted men, cadets, and foreign student pilots who served there
- Research Development Annex of A&M College
- Texas A&M Research Annex
- Bryan Research and Extension Center
- Riverside Campus

And now, the RELLIS Campus. Why "RELLIS?"

Let's let the visionary who came up with both the plan and the name explain himself.

Texas A&M University System Chancellor John Sharp:

> "We have Regent Cliff Thomas to thank for that.
>
> "About the time the A&M System took over what we now know as RELLIS, I asked Cliff, out of personal curiosity, how he remembered the 'core values' of Texas A&M. Cliff and I are both members of the Aggie Class of '72. While I was out knocking heads on the school's rugby pitch, Cliff played football at Kyle Field for Coach Gene Stallings.
>
> "The key element to that small piece of trivia is that Cliff wore a helmet to protect his head, while I did not. Thus, he tends to have a better memory than I do more than 40 years after we received our Aggie Class Rings.
>
> "Cliff told me he had created an acronym for the core values: RELLIS, standing for respect, excellence, leadership, loyalty, integrity, and selfless-service.
>
> "After giving that some thought, I called Cliff the next day and told him he had just named our new campus at the old Bryan Air Force Base.
>
> "I also ran the idea by Porter Garner, the president and CEO of the Association of Former Students. He told me, 'Man, that's great! Wonderful! Couldn't be a better name!'"

As any marketer will tell you, sustaining a consistent brand is important to business success. That "consistency," as it turns out, also makes for a more straightforward telling of history, something which RELLIS noticeably lacks.

"RELLIS Recollections," both the website and this book, is not intended to be a definitive, documented, nor detailed dissertation of RELLIS's diverse past.

This project *is* an attempt to capture and preserve the "essence" of the locale and the people whose contributions have made the place hallowed ground to many.

As you'll find from the video interviews on the website and the excerpted "In Their Words" sidebars within this book, the RELLIS history is precious to many, should be cherished by all . . . .and deserves to be investigated more deeply in the coming years.

I hope this project serves as a starting point for future historians.

I wish them well on their upcoming ventures.

For those of you looking for clarity, understanding, amusement, or to jog your memory of a nearby place but distant time, let me provide a brief overview of the principal chapters around which the RELLIS Recollections website is presented at rellisrecollections.org.

An understanding of that timeline should add to your enjoyment of the stories featured here—many of which first appeared in the "Brazos Life" section of *The Eagle* newspaper during the spring and summer of 2018.

Again, the RELLIS past can be a little confusing, given that it is just one place, but one place known by many names.

Local History (1821–Present)

The RELLIS Campus story predates its evolution from World War II military installation to 21st-century research and academic enclave. RELLIS not only carries on the Texas A&M core values from which its name is derived, but also springs forth from the enduring legacy of the State of Texas itself.

For those who come to RELLIS without an understanding of how Texas was shaped and why Texas is what it is today, this section of the website seeks to offer an overview of the local, regional, and state historic landscape.

The A&M College of Texas (1876–Present)

The school now known worldwide as Texas A&M University was first conceived in 1866. That year, the Texas state legislature accepted provisions of the Morrill Act, in which the United States Congress established "land-grant colleges" from the sale of federal lands and mandated investment accounts from the proceeds of those sales to provide for a permanent endowment to these newly formed institutions. Signed by Abraham Lincoln in 1862, the Morrill Act called for these schools to emphasize agricultural and engineering curriculum, as well as provide instruction in military tactics.

On April 17, 1871, the Agricultural and Mechanical College of Texas was established by the Texas state legislature. Appropriations of $75,000 were earmarked for construction and to hire faculty and staff. Some four and a half years later, on October 4, 1876, the school was dedicated on a site approximately 5 miles south of the town of Bryan.

That small parcel of land has grown into one of the world's preeminent and most tradition-rich institutions of higher learning.

Bryan Army Air Field (1942–1945)

The record suggests that nearly every man, woman, and child living in the Brazos County area turned out for the dedication of the Bryan Army Air Field on June 6, 1943. An estimated crowd of 25,000 people gathered at the base, located along State Highway 21 west of the city of Bryan. With the advent of US involvement in World War II, local business leaders and politicians waged skirmishes of their own to bring military bases and accompanying economic windfalls to cities and towns across the country.

Bryan, Texas, was one of those communities that "went to war."

As part of the 77th Flying Training Wing of the US Army Air Forces, some 5,000 pilots were trained at Bryan Field during the war. Bryan Field was home to the Army Air Forces' Instrumentation Instructors' School under the command of aviation pioneer Col. Joseph Duckworth.

The Annex (1946–1949)

Adjacent to Airfield Drive on today's RELLIS Campus sits a small plaza. The centerpiece of the commemorative space is a small block of granite upon which a plaque bearing these words rests:

> "Immediately after the end of World War II, the Agricultural and Mechanical College of Texas faced a severe housing and classroom space shortage because of the groundswell of returning veterans. Starting in 1946, facilities were leased at Bryan Army Air Field to house both returning veterans and incoming Corps freshmen classes. This effort produced 'The Annex' which became the first home of the four Aggie Classes of 1950, 1951, 1952 and 1953. They lived and studied here during their Fish years. The Aggies at 'The Annex' occupied more than 75 black tar-paper-covered single story barracks with a single common Mess Hall. Each barracks housed 20 students, had no air conditioning, and featured shared bathroom facilities.
>
> Approximately 5,500 Aggies inhabited 'The Annex' during those years and later graduated from the main campus in College Station. 'The Annex' was instrumental in producing over 4,000 officers for the Armed Services, 18 Distinguished Alumni, 28 General Officers, seven Presidents of the Association of Former Students, and two Regents for the A&M System.
>
> This plaque is dedicated to all of those Aggies who lived on 'The Annex'."

Bryan Air Force Base (1951–1958)

Shortly after the end of World War II, the US Army Air Forces was split into a separate branch of the military and renamed the United States Air Force. With the onset of the Korean War—and A&M freshman back full-time on the main campus—the air field grounds on the banks of the Brazos River was reactivated and renamed Bryan Air Force Base.

In the years between World War II and the Korean War, aviation technology advanced dramatically. Jet aircraft became the principle instrument of aerial warfare. To accommodate the new planes, more than $8 million was invested into the reopening of Bryan Air Force Base. Much of that money was used to facilitate the expansion of the post's main runways from 5,000 to 7,000 feet.

Research Annex (1962–1988)

In 1958, several years after the end of hostilities on the Korean peninsula, the General Services Administration declared the Bryan Air Force Base instillation surplus. Efforts were made to secure a buyer for the property both from the private and public sectors. Among those courted: both the cities of Bryan and College Station as well as the Brazos County board of commissioners. With an asking price of $18 million, no one could envision a means by which the venue could pay for itself, let alone be a money-making proposition.

Finally, a unique deal was struck with Texas A&M College. The agreement enabled the school to lease the property. Each year the site was used productively, 5 percent of the "purchase price" would be deducted. While the government retained the right to reactivate the base in case of national emergency, the plan enabled ownership of the site to transition to the university over a 20-year period . . . at virtually no cost.

Riverside Campus (1988–2016)

With full deed to the air base secured, Texas A&M—now officially known as a "university"—maintained a *status quo* at the Research Annex. While the Texas Engineering Extension Service and Texas Transportation Institute, state agencies that fell under the auspices of A&M management, maintained training and testing activities, the site's other principal use was to provide storage for the main campus. Little money was invested into improvements or infrastructure.

As the main campus enrollment grew sharply, there was a greater and greater need for new buildings to accommodate the rising student numbers. With an abundance of university-owned space at the old air base, the Texas A&M University System put together a study for how the locale could help address the growth.

Released in June 1988, the new master plan renamed the site as the "Riverside Campus" and provided a compelling need for change.

"For approximately 25 years, the former Bryan Air Force Base has served Texas A&M University as a location for research and extension activities which could not have been carried out on the Texas A&M University Main Campus. Plenty of space, both indoors and outdoors, has been available at low cost. Thousands of technicians and professionals have been trained at the site. Endless experiments have been conducted there and invaluable items have been stored there. However, the former Air Force base is burdened with an image problem, a seemingly remote location and an unattractive appearance. The 'Annex' is a place where few go, and then only out of necessity.

"The future should be different."

RELLIS Campus (2016–Present)

Little changed at Riverside for the next 20 years.

A second master plan was created in 2013 through the Center for Heritage Conservation. In the report, University Architect Lilia Y. Gonzalez saw the locale as a "21st century model for research and (an) education destination."

Finally, in 2016, Texas A&M University System Chancellor John Sharp determined the time was at hand for the Riverside Campus to enter the new era envisioned by Gonzalez and others through the years. Control of the venue was transferred to the System and Sharp gave it a new name: RELLIS.

What follows is an account covering 75 years, a promising future forged from a remarkable past.

The Fish Band got its start on the drill fields of Bryan Army Air Field, renamed "The Annex," as the first-year home of students within the A&M College Corps of Cadets in the years following World War II. Courtesy of Cushing Memorial Library & Archives, Texas A&M University.

CHAPTER 1
Skies Over the Brazos Valley

"In a sense, this school is a most unusual one, and is the only one of its kind."

In writing the foreword to the official—and once-classified—World War II "history" of Bryan Army Air Field, Colonel Joseph Duckworth chose his words carefully in providing an overview of the post whose command was his.

The word "history" suggests a retrospective view of events. In fact, Duckworth's Bryan Field history was a contemporary look at operations on the post and timed to be released on March 1, 1944, exactly one year after the base welcomed its first class of Army Air Forces' instructors as students to his school.

A young cadet in the Army Air Corps and then a commercial airline pilot, Duckworth was called back to active military service as the specter of German aggression in Europe blossomed into the Second World War. The new Army Air Forces charged Duckworth with a straightforward task: teaching American and Allied pilots to fly their planes safely through any kind of weather.

Left: T-6 Texan aircraft fly in formation over Bryan Field in ceremonies dedicating the facility in the late spring of 1943. Courtesy of Travis B. Bryan Family.

Bryan Field was the Army Air Forces' one and only Instrumentation Instructors' School.

In his foreword to the base history, Duckworth wrote:

> Only a few years ago flying an airplane, both in war and in peace, was little more than a sport. Today the modern airplane must be flown by instruments through all types of weather if it is to accomplish its mission. The mission of the airplane today is transportation, whether such transportation be that of passengers, freight or bombs. The pilot who cannot fly instruments today is only half a pilot.

Duckworth's Bryan Field story was put together under the watchful eyes of the post historian and intelligence officer, Captain Richard Sinz. Like Duckworth, Sinz had spent time in the military before there was a war to fight. As a civilian, he had managed the offices of the Retail Credit Company in San Antonio.

In his early 40s—the same age as Duckworth—Sinz began his duties at Bryan Field as a lieutenant, a product of both the Army Air Forces Officer Training School in Miami Beach, Florida, and the Intelligence School at Brooks Field in San Antonio.

Sinz would leave the war at the rank of colonel and return to San Antonio. He lived there the rest of his life until dying, at the age of 97, in 1995.

In his later years, Sinz was a member of the Austin Chapter of the Military Order of the World Wars, a "nonpartisan organization established as a means for officers of all military branches to come together to promote patriotic behavior, national security, good citizenship, and service to the United States."

An oral-history account of his time spent in World War II is contained within the archives of the Briscoe Center for American History on the University of Texas campus in Austin.

The written history of Bryan Field is detailed and complete, covering selection and construction of the site, duties and responsibilities of key personnel, mission and activities within the training curricula, and an analysis of the men and money it took to operate the instillation.

The estimated costs contained in the report to build out the base was approximately $6.5 million, of which $200,000 was used to construct "auxiliary landing fields" nearby in case of aircraft failure or pilot error. Those were located west of College Station, near Hearne, Texas, and at Easterwood Field.

By the end of February 1944, approximately 300 officers commanded nearly 2,400 enlisted men stationed at the base. So large was the civilian workforce needed at the airfield that a federal housing project near the post, called "Bryan Field Village," was built to accommodate those without living arrangements in the local area.

June 6, 2018, marked the 75th anniversary of the dedication of Bryan Army Air Field. No ceremonies took place as construction activities to prepare for the August opening of classes at Blinn College's new RELLIS Campus classroom building were in full swing at the former Bryan Field site. A full-page ad commemorating the anniversary did run in the local newspaper to little fanfare.

Bryan Field went "active" on March 1, 1943, with the arrival of the first instructor pilots to be trained in instrument flying. Construction was not yet complete.

Dedication of the field was pushed back to June 6 to accommodate the assembly of a P-51 Mustang funded by local donations and which would be given to the base for war-time use.

The real beginning of the RELLIS Campus story dates back to March of 1942. According to Sinz's history of Bryan Field, that is when Dr. T. O. Walton, then president of the Agricultural and Mechanical College of Texas, learned that Brazos County was "under consideration as a site for one of the fields" proposed by the Army Air Forces' Gulf Coast Training Center.

Walton mobilized key members of the local community to spearhead a campaign to bring a base to the local area. Local members of Walton's committee included a lumberman; two realtors; a county judge; the dean of A&M's College of Engineering, Gibb Gilchrist; Ivan Langford, the mayor of Bryan; and W. C. Mitchell, an insurance agent who was president of the Bryan Chamber of Commerce.

In the Bryan Field history, Sinz writes:

> After considering all phases of the (proposed area), a complete Site Board report was drawn up with recommendation to the Government that a tract of approximately 1875 acres be purchased in *fee simple* to be used as a station for an advanced single-engine school. The estimated cost of this land was $122,900.00 and it was owned by some forty-six individuals.
>
> On 5 August 1942 official establishment of the Army Air Forces Advanced Flying School, Bryan, Texas, was authorized by command of Major General Millard Harmon.

Construction began two days later and on September 24, the first "troops" arrived: four enlisted men from Moore Field in Mission, Texas.

Sinz wrote that the criteria most important in influencing the decision to build the base near Bryan included favorable climatic conditions, communication and transportation facilities, water and power supply, and "various off post facilities which would have an effect on military and civilian personnel."

This World War II era sign, reading “THE PILOT DEPENDS ON YOU,” remains in place on the RELLIS Campus today. Photo by author.

Built during construction of the original Bryan Army Air Field during World War II, the base chapel was a centerpiece of the site. And with death, a frequent companion to the activities which took place at the field, funeral services were often held here. Courtesy of US Army Air Forces.

The Army's insufficiencies in flying in inclement weather were brought to public attention during a nine-month period which became known as the "Air Mail Fiasco."

During the administration of President Herbert Hoover, Congress passed the Air Mail Act of 1930, giving commercial airlines the responsibility of ferrying mail for the US Government. Three years later, a Congressional investigation revealed that contracts were illegally awarded to only the nation's top commercial carriers.

In 1934, President Franklin Roosevelt rescinded the act and brought in the Army Air Corps to fly the mail.

But the military couldn't live up to the guarantee of "neither snow nor rain . . . staying these couriers from the swift completion of their appointed rounds."

By the late 1930s, an inability to fly safely in conditions of poor visibility resulted in several crashes along air-mail routes and the deaths of 13 airmen.

This unpleasant chapter in the annals of the Army Air Corps strengthened Joseph Duckworth's resolve to ensure American military pilots could—and would—fly safely in any kind of weather.

> The program is, then, to train pilots and instructors, not only in the technique of instrument flying, but how it should be taught by the latest methods. An important by-product of the program is the conversion of pilot training objectives to include proper training in instrument flying.
>
> Never again must the Army find itself in the position it was in when the air mail contracts were cancelled. From now on it must be prepared to fly any type of mission in any type of weather. To such a big objective this school is dedicated. The brilliant accident record and the statements of the graduates bear testimony to the fact that the goal is in sight.

Mastering the science—and art—of instrumentation flying was an important component in the Allied Forces gaining aerial superiority in the skies over both the European and Pacific theaters of the Second World War.

So vital to the war effort was Duckworth's command that the history of Bryan Field remained classified for nearly a decade. There are few photos of the base in wartime for that reason.

In fact, Duckworth's work was so important that he was absent for arguably the biggest day in RELLIS Campus history: the June 6, 1943, Bryan Field dedication. That event was engineered by a prominent local businessman absent from the citizen's committee that helped bring the installation to the local area.

Travis B. Bryan would become the major force in maintaining a military base—and its sizable payroll—in the town which his grandfather had helped create.

Gerald Ryan

When the US War Department chose to locate an Army Air Forces' installation west of the city of Bryan, a key reason was proximity to the Brazos River.

Access to water is an important element in forging the birth of any community, and Bryan Army Air Field would be a small city unto itself with a major need for water. That water did not come directly from the Brazos but from a sizable water table lurking under the river-bottom land where the installation was built.

Gerald Ryan grew up in Bryan and has retired there. His father, Charlie Ryan, worked on the crews that drilled the wells to serve Bryan Field. Gerald's mother, Bertie, would eventually work at the officer's club after the base was opened.

At the time, Gerald was a young boy completely fascinated by it all.

On the Lookout for German Spies

"My dad had drilled wells in the Brazos County area for many years and was one of the more experienced, better well-drillers. He worked for Jake Siegert at the time that he drilled the wells at Bryan Army Air Field.

"I remember that it was unusual to work on the night shift drilling water wells because that was always a daytime job. They did work day and night, and I figured that was an indication of the effort they made to expedite getting that military base up and running.

"I was born in 1932. So in 1942 (when construction on Bryan Field began) I was 10 years old and at that age you're very much interested in something like (the war).

"Pearl Harbor had just happened and I was interested in all the military and the airplanes and the tanks and all those kinds of things. I remember when I was out at Bryan Field on the night shift as a 10-year-old (with my father) wondering if there were German spies in the area seeing what we were trying to do there.

"So it was that kind of situation and that kind of tension with all the posters, you know, 'loose lips sinks ship' and all those kinds of situations. It was very much on everybody's mind. The war effort was all encompassing and it was a big part of everything that was happening locally.

"I lived on the west side of Bryan and, and after the air field opened, there were planes in the air just about all the time. It was the little A-T 6s and A-T 3s, the training planes, and they were real neat little planes. I spent a lot of time observing those and occasionally, but not real frequently, one would crash and they would have an account of that in the local newspaper. At that time there wasn't a lot of news happenings in the Bryan-College Station area. So, yeah, Bryan Field was pretty important to that time."

***Gerald Ryan** was born in Rock Prairie, Texas, in 1932. He graduated from Stephen F. Austin High School in Bryan. At the age of 18, Ryan went to work for the Southern Pacific Railroad as a telegrapher. While working the night shift, he enrolled at Baylor University, completing one semester there before transferring to Texas A&M. On his way to receiving a degree in marketing, Gerald proudly spent time tutoring members of Aggie football coach Bear Bryant's team. After graduation, Ryan went to work with the Owens-Illinois Glass Company and by the time of his retirement in 1988, he had risen to the position of general manager of the company's Dallas division. In 2016, he moved from New Mexico back to the Bryan-College Station area to be closer to family and friends.*

Courtesy of Gerald Ryan.

CHAPTER 2

The Godfather of Bryan Field

From the summer of 1942 until the end of World War II in 1945, the First National Bank of Bryan sold more than $5 million in war bonds to area businesses and residents.

That equates to $73 million today.

People wishing to back the global fight for freedom knew exactly where to go once they stepped through the front door of the bank, then located at 108 N. Main Street in downtown Bryan.

In front of the teller window where bonds could be purchased, bank president Travis B. Bryan anchored a Nazi flag to the floor. Treading across the black swastika symbolizing Germany's Third Reich led many donors to dig a little deeper into their pockets as a gesture of patriotic duty.

Bryan's war involvement—both the man's and the city's—did not stop there. The First National Bank board, chaired by Travis Bryan, played a vital role in supporting the area's newly opened US Army Air Forces' training base and the men and women who worked there, both in uniform and as civilians.

Construction on Bryan Field began in August of 1942. Over the course of the next two and a half years, the post pumped more than $9 million into the local economy, worth $132 million today. Although the base was deactivated at the end of World War II, Travis Bryan spearheaded efforts which saw the installation reopened at the outset of the Korean War.

Local banker Travis B. Bryan reads remarks at the dedication of Bryan Army Air Field on June 6, 1943. Courtesy of Travis B. Bryan Family.

Today, the site is known as the RELLIS Campus, and it owes much to the foresight and passion of one man.

Travis B. Bryan was born September 5, 1892, on a farm outside Giddings, Texas, about an hour southeast of Bryan. His parents, Erin and Nannie Bryan, instilled ambition into the youngest of their five children.

Travis's parents ultimately divorced and both died within a month of each other in 1910.

Travis Bryan's grandfather was William Joel Bryan, the namesake for the city of Bryan. The city's history dates back to 1860 when William Joel Bryan sold a one-square-mile tract of land to the fledging Houston and Central Texas Railroad. The city was incorporated in 1871.

Tim Bryan, chairman of The Bank & Trust of Bryan-College Station, is Travis B. Bryan's grandson.

"In 1886, my granddad's uncle, Guy M. Bryan II, co-founded what came to be known as The First National Bank of Bryan," Tim Bryan said. "Guy eventually sold his interest in the bank and moved to Houston to pursue opportunities there.

"A generation later, based on his own merits and his self-taught typing skills, my grandfather landed a job at that same bank . . . as a stenographer."

With the outset of American involvement in the First World War, Bryan left the bank and enlisted in the Army. He nearly died from illness while on active duty.

Of greater consequence to his future, Bryan witnessed the birth of aerial combat in the skies over Europe and emerged from his war experience a passionate proponent of building America's air power. When the Army Air Corps was established in 1929, he began methodically developing a network of contacts that ultimately reached the highest ranks of the military.

When World War I concluded, Travis Bryan returned to civilian life and his job at the First National Bank of Bryan. There, he quickly climbed the corporate ladder, becoming the bank's cashier in 1921. A dozen years later, he was a vice president and married to the daughter of bank president H. O. Boatwright.

When Boatwright died in August 1933, Bryan assumed the bank's helm.

After the Japanese attack on Pearl Harbor brought the United States into World War II, Travis Bryan saw an opportunity to serve both his country and his community at the same time. He was a staunch supporter of the ultimately successful effort to locate a military installation in the Brazos Valley.

"My granddad never ran for political office" said Tim Bryan, "but he was politically astute. He volunteered on numerous boards, panels, and committees and was well acquainted with a large swath of the Texas Congressional delegation in Washington."

Included in that group were Representatives William Poage, Albert Thomas, Sam Rayburn, and Lyndon Johnson.

By November of 1942, construction at Bryan Army Air Field was well underway. A small group of laborers working at the base wanted to contribute a day's pay to the government's war effort.

Such generosity was the norm of the time, but Travis Bryan saw that gesture as an opportunity to make a much larger statement.

On Tuesday, December 1, a full-page ad underwritten by the First National Bank of Bryan appeared in *The Bryan Daily Eagle* newspaper, which proclaimed "The Spirit of Bryan Field" as its headline.

"When the Japanese attacked Pearl Harbor in 1941," the ad stated, "in one day they made of America a united people with but a single purpose."

The ad was Travis Bryan's opening salvo in a campaign to raise $50,000 in donations for the purchase of a P-51 Mustang aircraft, which Bryan intended to donate to the Army Air Forces, as the Army Air Corps had come to be called.

The name of the proposed plane was to be *Spirit of Bryan Field*. In the newspaper ad, Travis Bryan asked all readers to donate their pay for the following Monday, December 7, the one-year anniversary of the Pearl Harbor attack.

Although Bryan Field was opened in March 1943, the official dedication wasn't held until June 6, 1943. Reasons for the delay were due to the "Spirit of Bryan Field" campaign. Assembly of the plane was delayed and delivery to Bryan Field pushed back to June 6.

On that day, the installation was dedicated and on behalf of those in attendance—whose numbers were reported to be close to 25,000—Travis Bryan presented the aircraft to the base's second-in-command, Major Arthur T. Leonard.

Brigadier General Luther Stevens Smith, a dashing West Point grad and commander of the 33rd Flying Training Wing, was the day's keynote speaker.

Four-year-old Annie Leonard, the major's daughter, christened the plane, needing multiple blows to uncap a bottle of Brazos River water against the propeller nosecone.

"Anyone who drinks from the Brazos River must return," Bryan told the throng, hoping to ensure that the newly minted aircraft would make it safely through the war.

According to the Air Force's Historical Records Agency, Travis B. Bryan's winged pride and joy never left the continental United States.

Army Air Forces documentation shows the aircraft was declared surplus and disposed as salvage less than two years after it first landed at Bryan Field.

Bryan Army Air Field's service to country ended, too, the price paid for US victory in World War II.

But, Travis B. Bryan saw a future for the encampment.

And, after all, he did have friends in high places.

New Bryan Air School Will Save Many Lives

June 7, 1943

BRYAN, TEXAS–(UP)—Army officers confidently predicted today that lives of many American fliers would be saved in the future because of a new flying school that has been opened here.

The school, formally dedicated yesterday before thousands of civilians, was organized for the sole purpose of giving better training to combat pilots who must fly in bad weather.

Instrument flying is an important part of modern aviation, but General Henry H. Arnold, commander of the Air Forces, believes that flying would be safer if this phase of it could be simplified.

> "Get an instrument system that these youngsters can understand," he told his officers one day, after he had read reports of two bombers that crashed while trying to get back to their base in a storm.

As a result of that order, a new system of training was developed largely through the work of Col. Joseph B. Duckworth, who at present is commanding officer of the field here.

In addition to dedication of the new school, yesterday also brought presentation of a new fighter plane, the gift of private citizens, to the Army. Bryan civilians raised the money for the plane and donated it to the government in appreciation of the work the air field is doing.

The plane, a Mustang fighter, was christened "Spirit of Bryan Field." It was christened with a bottle of Brazos River water in the hope that it would carry on a legend that anyone drinking of water from the Brazos River would return to the Brazos Country.

Scenes from the dedication of Bryan Army Air Field.

Above: *Spirit of Bryan Field* is stenciled onto the fuselage of a P-51 Mustang.

Top right: The speaking dais as seen from near the landing gear of *Spirit.*

Bottom right: Base visitors view the cockpit of a plane inside a hangar at Bryan Field.

Young Annie Leonard, daughter of one of Bryan Field's commanding officers, christens *Spirit of Bryan Field* with water from the Brazos River. Courtesy of Travis B. Bryan Family.

Pages 16–19 photos courtesy of Travis B. Bryan Family.

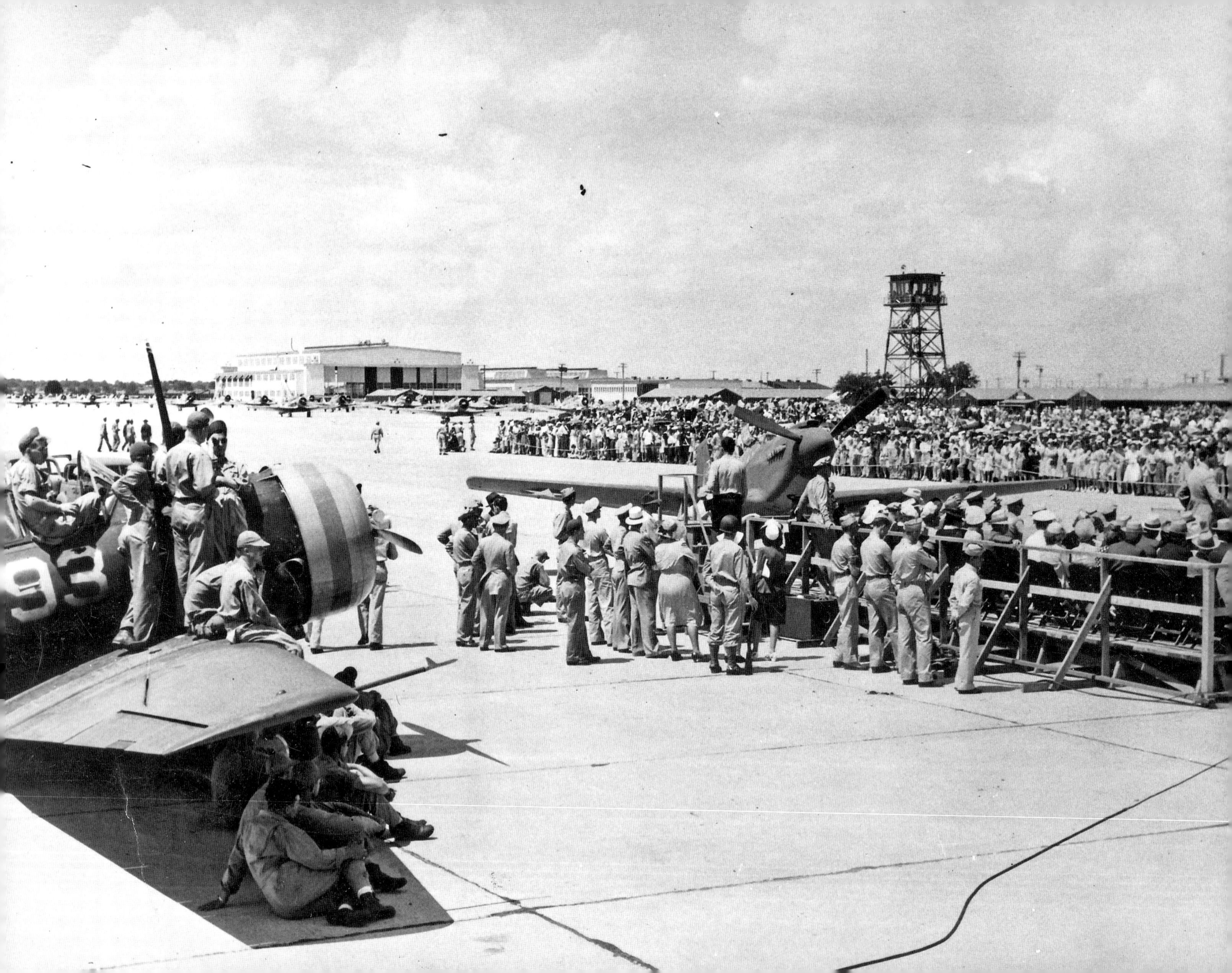
93

TRANSIENT AIRCRAFT
ELEV. 255

Travis B. Bryan (***left***), president of the First National Bank of Bryan, and one of the community's most fervent supports of a military presence in Brazos County. Courtesy of Travis B. Bryan Family.

CHAPTER 3
Letter to the President

(Note: This is an abridgment of an eight-page, single-spaced typewritten letter to the President of the United States, Harry Truman, by Bryan business leader Travis B. Bryan on Mother's Day, May 9, 1948).

Dear Mr. President:

For two weeks I have tried without success every day to address a letter to you which through the fortunate circumstances of the place of birth of yourself and a citizen of my community and a good friend and customer of my bank (Paul McDaniel) there is a good possibility that you may read.

For two weeks since he returned to Bryan from Washington and sat at the corner of my desk in the First National Bank of Bryan and told me of your cordial reception and of his willingness to present to you, the president of his and my country, a dream of my life, I have made several daily attempts to write you and without success.

I have destroyed countless pages of paper and all because even though you were born in the same town and have known Paul McDaniel and that he is welcome in your office and would in all likelihood be able to persuade you to listen to what I have to say frankly my brain becomes numb when I get to thinking of your job, of its responsibilities, of perhaps the impudence of my even contemplating taking up one moment of your valuable time.

This Sunday morning, Mother's Day, somehow after having breakfast with my good wife and seeing her off to her work in the Sunday School which for over 25 years she has enjoyed as superintendent of the intermediate department of the First Baptist Church in Bryan, (I'm a Scotch Irish Presbyterian, however, of a very poor caliber) I began to think of that love which passeth all understanding, of God's greatest gift to the human race, of the dear person that passed away thirty six years ago, my mother, but whose love has carried me through all the days of my life since and always will, and somehow after asking God's help on my knees in my bathrobe and slippers and in my home and with my personal typewriter, I have decided to try and write you of something that I think has such great possibilities for good for my country, my state, my community that I can do so as though I were writing not the President of my country, the man holding today the world's most important position, but just as one American

J. WEBB HOWELL, VICE-PRESIDENT
S. L. BOATWRIGHT, VICE-PRESIDENT
M. LINTON JONES, CASHIER

N. F. LOCKERD, ASSISTANT CASHIER
MELVIN C. JOY, ASSISTANT CASHIER
J. HOWARD TODD, ASSISTANT CASHIER

THE FIRST NATIONAL BANK

BRYAN, TEXAS

Mothers Day - May 9, 1948
Sunday Morning

Mr. Harry Truman
President of the United States
Washington, D.C.

Dear Mr. President:

For two weeks I have tried without success every day to address a letter to you which through the fortunate circumstance of the place of birth of yourself and a citizen of my community and a good friend and customer of my bank (Paul McDaniel) there is a good possibility that you may read.

For two weeks since he returned to Bryan from Washington and sat at the corner of my desk in the First National Bank of Bryan and told me of your cordial reception and of his willingness to present to you, the president of his and my country, a dream of my life, I have made several daily attempts to write you and without success.

I have destroyed countless pages of paper and all because even though you were born in the same town and have known Paul McDaniel and that he is welcome in your office and would in all likelihood be able to persuade you to listen to what I have to say frankly my brain becomes numb when I get to thinking of your job, of its responsibilities, of perhaps the impudence of my even contemplating taking up one moment of your valuable time.

This Sunday morning, mothers day, some how after having breakfast with my good wife and seeing her off to her work in the Sunday School which for over 25 years she has enjoyed, as superintendent of the intermediate department of the First Baptist Church in Bryan, (I'm a Scotch Irish Presbyterian, however, of a very poor calibre) I began to think of that love which passeth all understanding, of Gods greatest gift to the human race, of that dear person that passed away thirty six years ago, my mother, but whose love has carried me through all the days of my life since and always will, and some how after asking Gods help on my knees, and thinking of her on this her day being celebrated in our country, in my bathrobe and slippers and in my home and with my personal typewriter, I have decided to try and write you of something that I think has such great possibilities for good for my country, my state, my community that I can do so as though I were writing not to the President of my country, the man holding today the worlds most important position, but just as one American Citizen to another, and some how have confidence that not only may you read my letter (or brief) but that some how God in Heaven may cause you to do something about it.

\# 8.

When the day comes, and as surely as tomorrow's sun rises I am confident it will, that again I can stand with the commanding officer on the apron at Bryan Air Base and see 200 planes take off, fly prescribed courses and land perfectly, and the pilots raise the hoods that cover them; perhaps can attend commencement exercises at A&M and see a thousand young men trained and qualified step up and receive their commissions as Second Lieutenants in the Air Forces, well, I can look back to Sunday, May 9th, Mothers Day and remember this Sunday Morning and of writing you this letter and thank God that I was born in America, thank God for putting into my feeble brain such a life ambition, think of what good it can be or by that time may have been for my country, thank God for your having been born and those other friends I have been blessed with as mentioned herein.

As I did, I am sure that you did, that day returning from Europe when you steamed into the harbor of New York and saw the Statue of Liberty and the background of the buildings of New York, as you disembarked and saw the streams of cars, the evidence of wealth and power, the very way of life of our country, you as I thought above anything and everything else I am sure, THANK GOD FOR BEING AN AMERICAN.

As no other person can take the place of ones mother, as there is and never will be any other love such as a mothers love, as perhaps you will agree in all your life never anything that compares to that moment that the old Statue of Liberty came up over the horizon as you returned and I returned from Europe, in my life, some day to stand on the apron of the Bryan Air Base with it in active operation, well that day will be the second outstanding day of my life.

May God keep you and bless you and cause His face to shine upon you and cause you to side me in this program to the extent that you may immediately send word to Symington, Vandenberg, Spaatz and Cannon that you think immediate re-activation of Bryan Air Base and the institution of the training program makes sense.

Sincerely,

Travis B. Bryan, President.

Courtesy of Carnegie Library Collection.

Citizen to another, and somehow have confident that not only may you read my letter but that somehow God in Heaven may cause you to do something about it.

What I have been trying for years to do is to offer my country against some future day of need perhaps 1,000 young men every year who could instantly step into a rocket or jet propelled air plane at a moment's notice and go forth to defend our way of life.

And to offer that thousand expert pilots year after years as the years come virtually without it costing Uncle Sam a penny. Over the years, I have explained it day after day to men in high places, men qualified to estimate the value of the suggestion and without exception air I think I can assure you that so far not a single person has failed to agree with me. It has always been just a question of the proper time. From all indications the moment has arrived and all I need is that one person or several persons who are of a sufficient level of authority in our government to issue the instructions. What I am going to ask is that you interest yourself in the idea and indicate to the high level of the Air Forces your interest in it being done and on account of the world situation that it be done IMMEDIATELY.

I have in mind then and still have two ideas. For an air field to be set down at Bryan, Texas, to be bought and paid for in fee, that might last always and be a permanent part of the Air Forces program. That during the war every person stationed there might be treated by this community as an honored guest. That nothing the people of Bryan had would be too good for the personnel. An examination of the field's file in the Headquarters of the Air Forces will reflect that housing, services, and everything will bear out the statement that an unparalleled record was established, thousands of letters of the personnel still arriving daily in Bryan would attest it. In addition the people of Bryan joined in a program originated and sponsored by the First National Bank of Bryan, myself as its president, to CONTRIBUTE CASH AND BUY AND GIVE THE AIR FORCES a P-51, which was done before 25,000 people on the day of officially naming the field. I understand the next city in size to attempt the CASH ROUTE was Cleveland, Ohio. That's just one evidence of the spirit of this community.

You are familiar with the record of A&M an honor rated by the general staff of the Army ROTC military school, having produced more officers than any other school, and granted of equal calibre, in two wars in every branch of the service except NO AIR FORCE officers. In the air forces developing Bryn Air Base primarily for the instruction of its own personnel INCIDENTALLY with A&M College only 7 miles away it would be possible to obtain from this student body the men which in future years would develop 1000 2nd Lts in air forces reserve, a fresh crop every year, they could have four years of instruction at Bryan Air Base. You can take several thousand men and give them a few weeks training and make infantrymen of a sort out of them but it takes quite a few weeks to train a man to step into a rocket or jet propelled ship flying hundreds of miles an hour as a pilot and such trainees of Bryan Air Base through the 4 years of ROTC could be available.

I went overseas as a sgt. of ordnance in (the) first war. Just luck, nothing except I nearly died from double pneumonia and relapse but fortunate in that it prevented my going on the line where likely would have lost my life. Surely as the President of our country you cannot pass up the demand of our people for an air force as reflected in the recent action of the members of the congress.

What I'd like to ask you to do is to indicate that as the President of the United States you would favor the immediate activation of Bryan Air Base at Bryan, Texas, that the few millions to put the permanent brick buildings and modern equipment be set aside from the funds the congress has and will undoubtedly make available to them, so that this year by year incidental group of trained pilots can be available as well as training be given the Air Forces own personnel.

When the day comes, and as surely as tomorrow's sun rises I am confident it will, that again I can stand with the commanding officer on the apron at Bryan Air Base and see 200 planes take off, fly prescribed courses and land perfectly, and the pilots raise the hoods that cover them; perhaps can attend commencement exercises at A&M and see a thousand young men trained and qualified step up and receive their commissions as Second Lieutenants in the Air Forces, well, I can look back to Sunday, May 9th, Mother's Day, and remember this Sunday morning and of writing you this letter and thank God that I was born in America, thank God for putting into my feeble brain such a life ambition, think of what good it can be or by that time may have been for my country, thank God for your having been born.

Most humbly sir in deference and respect of the great position you hold, the responsibility thereof, would I direct this letter to you and in the utmost meekness ask God to cause you to think about it, read it, and then interest yourself in the program.

May God keep you and bless you and cause His face to shine upon you and cause you to side me in this program to the extent that you may immediately send word that you think immediate re-activation of Bryan Air Base and the institution of the training program makes sense.

Sincerely,
Travis B. Bryan, President

Tim Bryan

As the preceding letter suggests, Travis B. Bryan was determined in his quest to reopen the military air base in Bryan. Two years after his impassioned Mother's Day plea to the president, he assembled a 100-page document on why Bryan would be the ideal location for the newly conceived "academy" for the United States Air Force.

Those efforts, as his grandson, Tim Bryan, points out, ultimately paid dividends.

A Call From Harry

"My grandfather was chairman of the local Democratic Party. I'm not going to say he was a big 'politico,' but he was vitally interested in politics and stayed in touch with the people in Washington, DC, and even travelled up there for some inaugurations. His closest relationship was with Harry Truman, and I can see why because they were a lot alike. They were 'crusty.' They were both kind of crusty guys.

"My dad told me the story about when (my grandfather) lobbied to get the Bryan Air Force Base reopened for the Korean War. He traveled to Washington, DC, and met with all the secretaries of defense and secretary of the Air Force. He wanted it reopened.

"My dad was working in the bank one day in early 1951. My grandfather had gone off to play golf and there was a phone call that came in late that afternoon. My dad picked up the telephone and he answered, 'This is Travis Bryan,' and the voice on the other end said, 'Is this Travis Bryan? Wait, I'm looking for the old man.'

"My dad said, 'You're talking about my father,' and the voice on the other end said, 'Yeah, where is the 'SOB?' My dad said, 'Well, he's not here right now.'

"'Well, tell him to call me. This is Harry Truman,' which shocked my father, I'm sure.

"Dad hung up and ran out to the golf course and found my grandfather and brought him back to the bank where he called the president back.

"Truman had called to tell my granddad they had made the decision to reopen the Bryan Air Force Base—which was really good news for the city—and he wanted to personally tell him.

"My granddad was always buying and sending Stetson hats up to Washington, DC. So, some of the hats that Harry Truman famously wore were gifts from my grandfather. But granddad also gave them to the secretary of defense or anyone else that counted in Washington."

***Tim Bryan** serves as the chairman of the board and chief executive officer of The Bank & Trust of Bryan/College Station. A longtime banker, he's followed in the footsteps of his father, grandfather, and great uncle. His great-great grandfather was William Joel Bryan for whom the City of Bryan is named. Tim Bryan graduated from Texas A&M University in 1972. He began his business career in Houston, working his way up the ranks of Texas Commerce Bank. In the late 1980s, he purchased a series of Blockbuster video stores. He then sold those interests and moved back to Bryan in 1990. He is an avid historian and supports a wide range of causes in the local area.*

Courtesy of Tim Bryan.

CHAPTER 4
Neighbors for Life

Standing as a guest with Mary McCollom on the front porch of her tidy two-bedroom home on Luza Lane west of Bryan, one sees a small herd of Angus cattle grazing in a field of alfalfa grass on the other side of the road.

Beyond that to the south, vehicles traverse State Highway 21, barely audible in the half-mile distance, sparkles of light glimmering off their reflective surfaces.

And beyond that, looming above the horizon, a tower crane swings gently over the future headquarters of the Texas A&M Transportation Institute.

The building's interior blue shell rises four stories above the northern edge of what is now the Texas A&M University System's RELLIS Campus.

Seventy-five years ago, Mary looked from this same vantage point, or one much like it when her family's home sat in a slightly different spot, and witnessed construction of another kind.

The building of Bryan Army Air Field would bring the drama, excitement, and horrors of World War II nearly to Mary's front door.

Mary McCollom was but a young girl when she and her family moved to the farm on which she still lives.

How old was she at the time? Mary initially struggles for an answer.

Finally, she offers, "4-4-24" as a starting point. That's her date of birth, making her 94 years old as she watches the development of the RELLIS Campus.

Mary was about eight when her family, the Kalinecs, relocated to the place Mary continues to call home.

A wide range of emotions accompany Mary's recollections of days gone by.

Her parents and their four children moved from "town," in Bryan, to the country near the unincorporated communities of Smetana and Riverside in 1932.

She bristles at the remembrance of time spent picking cotton on the family farm. That was the cash crop of the river-bottom land on which the Kalinecs and their neighbors toiled. The Brazos River snakes a few miles to the west of her property, forming the Brazos-Burleson county line.

"For some reason it never flooded on this side," Mary recalls, "but on the west side, high water sometimes forced families onto the roofs of their homes."

A fonder memory for Mary is of a prized childhood doll, made from a corncob. She also remembers the pleasurable pursuit of penny candy.

Mary was 17 when the Japanese attacked the US Navy installation at Pearl Harbor, Hawaii. Today, she closes her eyes and can still see the ominous headlines for the event in *The Bryan Daily Eagle* newspaper.

Left: Photo by author.

She can still hear the bravado in the voices of the boys with whom she attended high school, not-yet young men ready for the adventure of war.

Locating a US Army Air Forces training facility in the Bryan area was a boon to the local community and its economy. But it required heavy sacrifice from some.

Nearly four dozen families around Riverside, many of whom Mary knew, lost their homes to the government's constitutional right of eminent domain.

The Kalinecs were fortunate. They kept their property.

It took only six months to build Bryan Field. Mary watched the progress on a daily basis. Thousands of pilots eventually trained at the site to become instructors. Thousands more worked in support of those training efforts.

Many of those individuals were young—not much older than Mary—and experiencing the most thrilling time of their young lives. Mary lived close enough to be caught up in the wonderment.

"From dawn to dusk, planes were flying everywhere," says Mary. She didn't think of it at the time, but those planes flew in both good weather and bad.

Sometimes those planes crashed and people died.

Bryan Field was the Army Air Forces' principal instrumentation-flying school. The work was demanding.

Play, or "morale-boosting activities" as the Army called it, was equally intense.

"All along Highway 21, dance halls and clubs sprang up," Mary says, "catering to the military personnel."

West of her home, the county line created an important divide.

"Brazos County was dry," Mary explains. "If you were a member at a 'club,' you could get a beer. But across the river in Burleson County, they served liquor by the drink."

The Highway 21 span linking Brazos and Burleson counties is still called "Whiskey Bridge."

"A lot of those boys were wild!" Mary's eyes light up at the recollection. "Some nights, the ladies would have to hide behind the jukebox to avoid all the flying bottles!"

At a place called The Night Spot, 19-year-old Mary Kalinec met Louis Massey, a young airman from Clay County, Arkansas. One of Mary's aunts, her own husband fighting the war in some faraway place, enjoyed the social goings-on in proximity to Bryan Field. She often asked Mary to accompany her.

Mary and Louis quickly became a couple. That happened a lot around Bryan Field.

"Louis was funny and friendly and I hated working in the cotton fields," Mary says of the things she found most attractive about her new beau. That and his attire. "Louis didn't fly," Mary says. "He worked on planes. But all those boys looked pretty special in their dress uniforms."

And none of them had cars.

"When they had a pass, a lot of the boys would leave the base on foot," Mary says. "Some of them ventured as far as our road, but my parents didn't want me to talk to any of them.

"I guess that changed when I started seeing Louis."

She laughs at the memory of late weekend nights in which she and her aunt were able to "smuggle" Louis back on base with him hiding in the trunk of a car, past sentries who looked the other way thanks to a girlish wink and a smile.

Both Mary and her sister, Shirley, wound up marrying enlisted men from Bryan Field. Shirley's husband, "Tex," was from Corsicana.

Mary and Louis moved next door to her parents, still within proximity of the family's cotton field where Mary continued to toil during the picking season. The couple had one child.

Louis Jr., who goes by "Sonny" today, was born on December 6, 1944.

After the war, Louis Sr. continued training as an aircraft mechanic and worked as a civilian at Bryan Air Force Base when the installation was reactivated for the Korean War. When the base was permanently closed in 1958, Louis had difficulty finding steady employment. Ultimately, he and Mary divorced and he moved back to Arkansas.

She remarried and has outlived both husbands.

During the peak of training activity at Bryan Air Force Base, planes occasionally "fell from the sky," as Mary describes it today.

Sonny, too, has vivid recollections of the vagaries of war coming a little too close for comfort.

"My grandfather was setting salamander traps in his sweet potato patch," Sonny recalls of a day still vivid from his childhood memory.

"I was outside playing when all of a sudden I heard this roar, looked up and saw an airplane flying dangerously low to the ground.

"It was headed straight toward my granddad. He saw it, too, and started running.

"The plane hit the ground and the front landing gear broke. The propeller dug into the dirt and the plane flipped completely over.

"Otherwise, I think it would have killed my grandfather."

Miraculously, the pilot also survived the crash, but death was frequently the outcome of aerial mishaps around Bryan Air Force Base.

"One time they killed one of our cows," Sonny recalls.

"I don't remember exactly what happened, but the Air Force reimbursed us for the loss."

Mary McCollom, grandson James Massey, great-grandson Creed Dotson, son Sonny Massey, and granddaughter Sheila Dotson. Photo by author.

Charles and Regina Opersteny

The US War Department's seizure of nearly 2,000 acres of property west of Bryan, Texas, to establish what would become known as the Bryan Army Air Field impacted lives. Almost four dozen landowners were effected. Their "just compensation" for the Brazos River bottomland was $122,000 . . . total. It is said that some of those affected refused payment, hoping the land would revert back to their ownership after the war.

That did not happen.

Charles and Regina Opersteny grew up in Bryan and both spent time working at the site of Bryan Field during the Korean War. Not yet married at the time, Charles was on active duty at Bryan Air Force Base as a medical corpsman, while Regina held a civilian clerical job there.

Some 60 years later, the Operstenys live on the Stetz family farm where Regina grew up. Their home is just 3 miles south of the RELLIS Campus. Today, the homesite is a perfect retreat for the loving couple who have been active in community affairs in the local area most of their adult lives. But, as Regina remembers, there was a time when a pall hung over the property as the government prepared to exercise its right of eminent domain to build Bryan Army Air Field.

"Not in My Backyard"

Regina Opersteny: "The citizens of Bryan really were excited about it, but my parents weren't because we were nervous. It was too close to us. In fact, it could have been us. My family bought this place when they came over from Europe, and it's been ours since 1878, so we were very nervous about it.

"I remember visiting a family and they had to move with their home, well situated, but of course the US government bought them another

***Charles and Regina Opersteny** are Bryan natives. They attended high school together and started dating while both were at Bryan Air Force Base. Regina Stetz served in a civilian clerical position, while Charles was a medical corpsman in the US Air Force. He went on to become a Bryan/College Station physical therapist. He remains active in Bryan's American Legion Post 159. The couple lives on Regina's family farm located near the old Bryan Air Force Base site.*

Photo by author.

place. Still, they had to find it and it was kind of an emotional thing to leave your home.

"And that was one of the things that my parents and my grandmother, she was still living at the time, were worried that this place was going to be taken up, too. But thank goodness it wasn't. As they say, 'Not in my backyard, go somewhere else.' But when I went to work there, I was glad it was there."

Charles Opersteny: "I went into the service in December of 1950 and started my basic training at Lackland Air Force Base outside of San Antonio. They then rounded up a bunch of us and shipped us over to Randolph Air Force Base to finish our basic training. Randolph was the 'mother base' to Bryan, and I wound up being one of the first people sent here after they reopened the base in 1951. I spent a lot of time doing carpenter work at the old hospital for a tech sergeant who was also a pharmacist and in charge of fixing up the facility. After that I became a corpsman working in the dispensary, which involved some treatment of patients. We had a whirlpool and I helped with rehabilitation.

"My parents' home was on the west side of Bryan and I spent some time there, but on base, I lived in one of the barracks. In fact, I was in charge of the barracks where I lived. It was a single-story old World War II structure. Latrines were out behind it, so you had to go outside to use the latrine and take a shower."

Regina: "I worked in the big hangar next to where they repaired the aircraft and, as a result, I got interested in planes. I ordered parts for the mechanics—that was my job. Sometimes, when we didn't have a part at the base supply, I would have to make arrangements to have that part shipped to Bryan from the depot in San Antonio. I worked there for three years, much longer than Charles was stationed there, and I enjoyed the work very much. I enjoyed working with all the civilians as well as the service men there."

A T-6 Texan, similar to the plane Colonel Joseph Duckworth flew twice into a hurricane. Courtesy of US Army Air Forces.

CHAPTER 5

Hurricane Hunter

The world's first "hurricane hunter" made his maiden voyage from a rather unlikely place and with an even more unlikely rationale.

In fact, the pilot had to go find the storm rather than the storm coming to him.

The first "intentional expedition" into the midst of a tropical tempest was launched from the runways of Bryan Army Air Field in the summer of 1943.

Literally on a dare, the pilot guided a single-engine propeller-driven military training aircraft into a Category-2 storm off the Texas Gulf Coast near Galveston. He did so without approval or authorization from his superior officers.

And then, later that same day, he flew back into the storm a second time.

At the helm on those history-making missions was Colonel Joseph Duckworth, the commander of Bryan Field and the man charged with leading the Army Air Forces' efforts to teach war-time aviators to remain aloft when flying through inclement weather based solely on the readings of the instrument panels in their aircraft.

Duckworth's regimen helped the United States win the war, but no one was ever expected to fly through hurricane conditions. Still, his hurricane flights from Bryan Field made Duckworth a legend . . . in certain circles.

John Nielsen-Gammon is a Regents Professor at Texas A&M University and the Texas State Climatologist. He knows Duckworth's story well.

"What he accomplished is the meteorological equivalent of a trip to the moon," Nielsen-Gammon said.

Amazing to Nielson-Gammon is that Duckworth made his flights with no preparation. Rather, he may have simply let his emotions get the better of him.

"It was a bar bet," Nielsen-Gammon said. "More accurately, it was a wager made over coffee in the morning mess hall at Bryan Field."

The National Oceanographic and Atmospheric Administration calls the weather system which struck the Texas coast on July 27, 1943, the "Surprise Hurricane."

Wartime fears of German U-boat activity in the Gulf of Mexico mandated that all friendly ships there maintain radio silence. In an era before radar and satellite imagery, the US Weather Bureau relied almost exclusively on radio transmissions from ships at sea for its off-shore forecasting information.

So unexpected was the storm that struck the Texas coast in the summer of 1943 that 19 people died in its path with hundreds more injured.

Colonel Joseph Duckworth, (*left*). Courtesy of US Army Air Forces.

When news of the hurricane reached Bryan Field, base personnel scrambled to secure all aircraft.

Bryan Army Air Field was home to the Army Air Forces' Instrumentation Instructors' School. Duckworth's mission there was to train trainers in the technique of full-instrumentation flying.

Before Duckworth, Army pilots flew a rudimentary "1-2-3" methodology when visibility deteriorated during flight, using only the turn, ball-bank, and airspeed indicators on their display panel. In the early years of World War II, more lives and aircraft were lost to inclement weather than actual combat.

Duckworth, a native of Savannah, Georgia, enlisted in the US Army Air Corps in 1927 at the age of 25. He received his flight wings and a reserve commission while stationed at Kelly Field, near San Antonio.

As a civilian, Duckworth later flew for Ford Motor Company and then Eastern Airlines.

Piloting commercial aircraft for 10 years—with paying customers to ferry through clear or overcast skies—Duckworth gained an all-encompassing understanding of full-instrumentation flight.

In 1940, Duckworth was called to active military duty and charged with changing the way Army pilots flew in bad weather.

Duckworth was initially stationed in Columbus, Mississippi. Then, after Pearl Harbor, plans were made for a dedicated instrument instructor's school. That facility was located at Bryan Field.

A group of British aviators were among the cadre of students there in July of 1943.

"The Brits, who were used to storms raking the coast of England, were amused at the prospect of the Americans having to get their 'fragile' aircraft out of the way of the impending hurricane," said Nielsen-Gammon. "I'm not certain they understood what damage a hurricane could actually do, but Colonel Duckworth took offense.

"So he wagered his comrades he could fly into the hurricane, come back, and remain unscathed."

Lieutenant Ralph O'Hair was the only flight navigator on the field that morning. Sitting at the mess table with Duckworth and the British pilots, he was drawn into the debate.

When Duckworth turned to ask O'Hair if he would navigate the impromptu mission, the lieutenant agreed.

"Such was my respect for Duckworth and his flying abilities," O'Hair would later say.

As commander of the field, Duckworth was the ultimate local authority. But he had superior officers elsewhere to whom he reported.

He knew approval was impossible, both because of the risk to man and machine and the amount of time it would take to escalate the request up the chain of command.

The storm wouldn't wait.

Duckworth and O'Hair took off.

"While everyone else was trying to run away from the storm, Duckworth was flying toward it," Nielsen-Gammon said. "When they made radio contact with Houston air-traffic control, they were told to keep close track of their position so that search parties could be sent out for rescue when the plane disappeared."

Sitting behind Duckworth as he flew through the heavy rains contained in the outer bands of the storm, O'Hair pondered what it would be like to parachute into a hurricane. He remembered "being tossed about like a stick in a dog's mouth."

Then suddenly, all was quiet.

They had entered the eye of the storm.

Above them bright clouds appeared. Below, they could see land. O'Hair estimated the diameter of the eye to be 9 or 10 miles. He described the shape of the center as a "leaning cone." Duckworth circled inside the storm's calm interior for a time.

Aligning the aircraft toward home, Duckworth punched his plane back into the hurricane for the return flight to Bryan Field. Again he met torrential rainfall and gusting winds.

Still, his confidence in flying through such conditions was never shaken.

Upon landing back at Bryan Field, there was little time to celebrate. The field's weather officer, Lieutenant William Jones-Burdick, was standing on the flight line.

"Burdick requested permission to go back into the storm," Nielsen-Gammon said.

"So, after making the first intentional flight into a hurricane, Duckworth then made the first scientific flight on the same day."

That night on post, the achievements were celebrated. Never again would anyone doubt the durability of the North American Aviation-made T-6 Texan, which was the primary training aircraft at Bryan Field.

Within a year, the US Army Air Forces established a Weather Reconnaissance squadron. By 1946, those who flew missions for that group were officially called "Hurricane Hunters." They still fly today as the 53rd Weather Reconnaissance Squadron of the Air Force Reserve.

Duckworth retired from the Air Force in 1955 and became head of the safety bureau of the Civil Aeronautics Board. He died on July 26, 1964, in Battle Creek, Michigan, one day shy of the 21st anniversary of his historic flights.

Each year, the US Air Force presents an award in Duckworth's honor recognizing contributions to aerospace instrument flight.

An historical marker outside the east entrance to the RELLIS Campus details Duckworth's remarkable wartime achievement.

Joe Williams

Unquestionably, Joseph Duckworth saved American lives and helped Allied Forces win World War II. He did so by instilling within the entirety of the US Army Air Forces—from fighter planes to transport carriers to bombers—a commitment to proficiency of flying aircraft based solely on the information to be gathered from the readings of their cockpit control panels.

That did not mean that his training base in Bryan, Texas, was a safe place. On the contrary, there was an extreme sense of urgency in the mission at the site. So focused was Duckworth on the job at hand that he mandated a reduction in administrative officers at his instillation. And, in fact, Bryan Army Air Field had the lowest percentage of officers devoted to administrative functions, less than 18 percent, of any Army Air Forces instillation in the country.

Danger in Bryan could be found in the most—and least—unlikely places. Former Texas A&M University System architect Joe Williams' brother trained at Bryan Field, and after surviving dozens of combat missions in Europe, he suffered his most serious mishap . . . on the ground.

Brother's Peril

Joe Williams: "My brother was Lieutenant Norman Williams. His nick-name was Pete. Everybody called him Pete. He flew 59 missions in Europe in medium bombers and they assigned him back to the United States and sent him to Bryan Air Base for instrument training.

"While he was here one morning he was in a trainer in the back seat, under what they call the hood, so he couldn't look out and see what was going on. But he knew there were two lines with planes on the runway and he was in one line and then there was another line next to them. And instead of using a radio for some reason, they decided to use a green light from the tower and the first plane would receive the green light, pull to the middle of the runway, and take off. Then they'd give a green light to the next one.

"Well, with all the engines running there was a lot of noise. Pete said all of a sudden there was a grinding of metal and then he felt a big bump. He looked up and here's a propeller blade coming down right in front of his face. Apparently two guys got the take-off signal at the same time and ran together. Fortunately, no one was hurt."

*Now retired, **Joe Williams** serves as a volunteer at the George H.W. Bush Presidential Library on the campus of Texas A&M University. For more than 15 years, from 1983 to 1999, Williams worked in the Facilities Planning Division of the Texas A&M University System. Williams earned his undergraduate degree in architecture from the University of Florida and worked along the Atlantic Coast as an architectural professional until taking a job with the firm Lockwood, Andrews and Newman in Houston in 1977. There, he worked on several football stadium renovation projects, including the University of Oklahoma's Memorial Stadium and Texas A&M's Kyle Field.*

Courtesy of Joe Williams.

RELLIS Recollections: Now, that sounds like everybody was in a big hurry and I guess that big hurry had to do with preparing for the invasion of Japan.

JW: "Yeah. This is what it was all about. They were trying to get everybody ready and trained again to go to the Japanese Pacific War. And, fortunately they didn't have to go."

RR: . . . with the dropping of the atomic bombs ending World War II. Now, how did you wind up here in the Bryan-College Station area, because you and your brother weren't originally from this part of the country.

JW: "No, we were both from Florida. I went to school and became a registered architect and worked several places around the country because architecture is part of construction and you have to go where the people are building things in order to have the business.

"I ended up in Houston and spent six years there, and, fortunately, one of the first jobs they gave me at the firm I was working for was to study the possibility of adding a third deck to Kyle Field at Texas A&M. It turned out it was feasible and so they gave me the job as project manager to get the design work done on that and I got to know the people at Texas A&M and, over a period of time, I became employed with the same people here at A&M. It was a very good experience."

RR: In that job, you actually did some work out here at what's now the RELLIS Campus, right?

JW: "Yes. At that time, of course, it was called Riverside Campus and it was primarily used for TEEX (Texas A&M Engineering Extension Service) and for TXDOT (Texas Department of Transportation). At TTI (Texas A&M Transportation Institute) they did a lot of 'experimental' work for TXDOT. One of my projects out here was to design a laboratory, like a training class for testing people and their driving ability at certain alcohol levels. We all volunteered to be the 'designated drunk,' but they didn't accept any of us."

Wayne Sadberry, *left*, curator of the Brazos Valley African-American Museum, shows Greg Winfree, agency director for the Texas A&M Transportation Institute, the house in Bryan that Sadberry's uncle leased to Captain John Porter. Photo by author.

CHAPTER 6
Tuskegee Airmen

> ***"The world's greatest democracy fought the world's greatest racist with a segregated Army."***

So writes acclaimed historian Stephen Ambrose in his book, *Citizen Soldiers*.

And, while Adolph Hitler fought World War II on three fronts—Western, Russian, and Holocaust—African American soldiers fought both the enemy abroad and a prevailing Jim Crow mindset at home.

At least in southern states . . . like Texas.

The Texas A&M University Press published *Black Soldiers in Jim Crow Texas, 1899–1917* more than 20 years ago. In the work, author Garna Christian writes of a 1917 clash in Houston between black troops and white locals.

Fifteen people died in the confrontation. Dozens more were injured.

A story in the *Burleson County Ledger*, dated April 9, 1943, suggests the racial divide remained vast during our nation's involvement in the Second World War.

"There are several hundred Negroes stationed at Bryan Field," the Caldwell-based paper reported, "but so far as this column is aware, not one of these men has been given leave into Bryan."

A story three months later in the Baltimore *Afro-American* newspaper quoted a hometown soldier as saying he and his fellow black service-men were being treated "worse than dogs" at Bryan Field.

The unidentified individual continued, "We had five sergeants and eight corporals when the 325th (Aviation Squadron) came to this field, but they have all been busted because they wanted to transfer to other camps on account of bad treatment."

Colonel Joseph Duckworth, the base commander, was a son of the South. He was born in Savannah, Georgia, and in 1940 was called to active military duty from a job in Atlanta as a commercial airline pilot with Eastern Airlines.

He took command of Bryan Field, the Army Air Forces only instru-ment pilot instructor's school.

Captain Elwood T. Driver was one of the thousands of pilot-instructors to successfully complete Duckworth's "all-weather" instrumentation course. He finished the six-week program in January 1945.

His involvement and success is historically notable.

Driver was the first "colored officer"—as proclaimed by a news release from the Public Relations Office at Bryan Field—to gain instrument rating at the Texas installation.

He was also a Tuskegee Airman.

The Tuskegee Airmen were, famously now, the first black military aviators in US history.

Eugene Bullard was the first American Negro to serve as a military pilot. Rejected for aerial duty by the US Army, he flew with the French Air Service during World War I.

On April 3, 1939, Congress, for the first time, appropriated funds for the training of black pilots for Army Air Forces duty. The War Department's criteria for black candidates was far more stringent than for white prospects.

In a still segregated Army, those training funds were funneled to civilian flight schools with the expectation of creating an even broader crevasse for blacks wanting to fly.

It turned out one of the flight schools funded by the act was at the historically black Tuskegee College in Alabama.

The Tuskegee Army Air Forces' program began in June 1941. Nearly a thousand pilots successfully earned their wings there. More than 350 were deployed overseas.

Eighty-four Tuskegee Airmen died in service to their country.

The Tuskegee aviators acquitted themselves brilliantly. Their performance, in part, led to Executive Order 9981, in which President Harry Truman abolished racial discrimination in the US Armed Forces in 1948.

Before arriving at Bryan Field, Driver had flown more than 120 combat missions in the Mediterranean region of the European theater of war. He earned, among other citations, an Air Medal with Clusters and the Distinguished Flying Cross.

A native of Trenton, New Jersey, Driver had sought to attend the US Naval Academy in the years leading up to World War II.

But, despite scoring the highest mark on the academy's admittance test, Driver was not accepted. According to his page on the Smithsonian National Air and Space Museum website, he flunked his physical for "overlapping teeth."

Driver joined the Tuskegee Airmen in 1942. He retired from the Air Force as a major in 1962. He's included on the Tuskegee Airmen's "Wall of Honor" at the National Air and Space Museum in Washington.

In 1978, President Jimmy Carter appointed Driver to the National Transportation Safety Board, where he eventually became vice chairman.

When Bryan Air Force Base was reactivated in 1951, one of the first instructor pilots assigned there was another Tuskegee Airman, First Lieutenant John Porter.

Porter was born in Cleveland and after the war made Dover, Delaware, his family's home. The Tuskegee Airmen, Inc. Delaware chapter is named in his honor.

When Porter was assigned to Bryan, he was encouraged to find off-base housing for his family. Quarters for married officers were limited.

Despite later promotion in rank to captain, Porter's options for residence in the city were restricted too. Bryan was a segregated community, and Porter was forced to live in the segregated part of town.

He and his family wound up renting a home near the corner of 18th and Hall in Bryan. The house was owned by Charles Sadberry, whose nephew, Wayne Sadberry, today serves as curator of the Brazos Valley African American Museum in Bryan.

"I remember Capt. Porter," Sadberry says with a smile. "He was flashy and liked fast cars.

"But then, that described every pilot who came through Bryan Air Force Base."

Sadberry has lived in Bryan his entire life. He's experienced intolerance and compassion. He's seen both the toll ignorance can take and the fruits that come from understanding.

"I can't say I ever had a chance to sit down and talk with Capt. Porter," Sadberry says. "But, I knew he was a Tuskegee Airman, and even as a boy I grasped that they were heroes in every sense of the word."

Gregory Winfree is another lifelong admirer of the Tuskegee legacy.

Winfree is among the Texas A&M System's highest ranking African Americans. He serves as agency director for the Texas A&M Transportation Institute and was a former assistant secretary in the US Department of Transportation during President Barak Obama's administration.

"My dad knew several of the Tuskegee Airmen who settled near our home on Long Island," Winfree says.

"I've inherited my father's respect and admiration for those men. So much so that I'll be painting the tail of my motorcycle red, making me a 'Red-Tail' motorcycle gang of one here in the Bryan-College Station area!"

The Tuskegee Airmen's planes, most notably P-51 Mustangs, were painted with red noses and tails to ensure they were easily identifiable in aerial combat and a more visible distraction on their famed bomber-escort missions during World War II.

Winfree took the helm of the Texas A&M Transportation Institute in December 2016. As he's learned about the history of the old Bryan Army Air Field—on which site much of the Texas A&M Transportation Institute's research work is conducted and its headquarters operations will be located—Winfree has developed a sense of pride regarding the venue's Tuskegee connection.

"I feel a particular bond with Major Driver," Winfree explains. "After his military career, he was a trailblazer at the US Department of Transportation.

"In fact, he earned the DOT's Special Achievement Award in 1975.

"I came along to the department much, much later," adds Winfree, "but I can tell you, I'm honored to have followed in his footsteps."

Gregory Winfree and Wayne Sadberry admire a page from a 1952 Bryan Air Force Base yearbook in which then First Lieutenant John Porter was recognized for his artistic contributions to the publication. Photo by author.

Captain John Porter with his 52-D "Comet Flight" cadets at Bryan Air Force Base. Courtesy of US Army Air Forces.

John Porter. Courtesy of US Army Air Forces.

Elwood Driver. Courtesy of US Army.

BAFB yearbook page saluting Porter's contributions and two of his illustrations contained in the publication.

Courtesy of US Army Air Forces.

Courtesy of US Army Air Forces.

Greg Winfree

Since December 2016, Greg Winfree has served as agency director for the Texas A&M Transportation Institute. Much of TTI's research work is conducted on the RELLIS Campus and has been for more than 50 years.

A trial lawyer by training, Winfree is also an avid student of history. He grew up on Long Island and has vivid recollections of his father's tales of the famed Tuskegee Airmen, the pioneering corps of black Army aviators who served their country with distinction in World War II.

Tuskegee Airmen were the Winfree's neighbors, having served at Long Island's Mitchell Field both during and after the war and then remaining in the New York City region.

Given that Tuskegee Airmen dotted the landscape at both Bryan Army Air Field and Bryan Air Force Base during the 1940s and 1950s, Winfree has a keen sense of pride in the fact his agency shares a history with the famed aviators.

But what of the role the Tuskegee Airmen played in forging opportunities for black men like Winfree in today's America?

The Tuskegee Legacy

"That era of global conflict, World War II, forced all parties, all citizens together, really for the first time. History proves that whenever we, as a people, have a common enemy, we tend to be at our best when the focus is in the same direction. During World War II, that was true of blacks and women as well. Women played a significant role in the war effort, too. Thus, the racial and gender divides, at least within the military, blurred some.

"Can you imagine working in an environment where on the inside everyone is pretty much treated as equals, but on the outside, when you leave your job, you're thrust back into this other tiresome and foreboding world?

"My father, Walter Winfree Jr., was a successful business executive and entrepreneur. But, he, too, experienced a racial divide in his military career when he was stationed at Fort Huachuca near Sierra Vista, Arizona, in the 1950s. That's the outpost the US Army established in its 'war' on Geronimo in the late 19th century, and the same place that became home to the 'Buffalo Soldiers,' the all-black cavalry regiment that was the spiritual forefathers of the Tuskegee Airmen in the years leading up to World War I.

"Sierra Vista, like Bryan, Texas, in the middle years of the 20th century, was a segregated community. In the case of Sierra Vista, a mining town, there were no blacks and no Hispanics. My dad grew up

***Greg Winfree** has served as Agency Director of the Texas A&M Transportation Institute since December 2016. Greg joined the US Department of Transportation's Office of the Assistant Secretary for Research and Technology in March 2010 as Chief Counsel and was later sworn in as Assistant Secretary for Transportation in January 2014. He received a JD from Georgetown University and previously served as corporate counsel for several Fortune 500 corporations.*

Courtesy of the Texas A&M Transportation Institute.

in New York, and it was a challenging transition for him to be stationed at a place where people not only were telling him what he could and could not do with his free time but also, and more dramatically, who he was.

"That didn't set well with my father, and so he demanded a meeting with his commanding officer to discuss the unfair treatment of both the black and Hispanic soldiers at the post. The story sort of ends there. I don't recall whether any significant changes were made, but it says a lot about my father that he was willing to put himself on the line for what he believed.

"And while it may not be as overt today, many of those same problems, that same racial divide, still exist.

"I've always been a big fan of war movies. And in many of those films, the brave soldiers were usually just one color and that wasn't my color. My dad would always pepper conversations with comments like, 'Don't forget, "we" were there, too.' That's what made meeting those former Tuskegee Airmen on Long Island so important to me. These 'heroes' would come around dressed in their flight jackets and with their decorations and talking about their time spent in service to our country. For a boy like me, it was critical to understand that people who look like me played an important role in our country's history.

"I've been proud to serve my country, too, and I've been fortunate to do so under two presidential administrations. I was a young trial attorney in the Civil Rights Division of the Department of Justice under President George H.W. Bush, and later an assistant secretary in the US Department of Transportation under President Barak Obama.

"And, yes, I've been a recipient of, let's call it, 'disparate treatment," because I'm black. But I'm also a lawyer by training and that means I'm pretty good at researching the 'facts.' And maybe that's where things are a little different today. When you get down to it, for the most part, there's no denying the facts. At the end of the day, I've always been able to make a pretty compelling case because I know how to do my job.

"And people, regardless of color, usually respect that."

Suzanne DeLano (***middle***) and Joan Michaels (***second from right***) were the only two WASPs stationed fulltime at Bryan Army Air Field during World War II. Courtesy of Texas Woman's University, Woman's Collection.

CHAPTER 7
WASP

On Saturday night, May 26, 2018, at Avenger Field in Sweetwater, Texas, a sellout crowd of more than 300 attended a dinner and memorial service at the National WASP World War II Museum. The event marked the 75th anniversary of the Women Airforce Service Pilots and celebrated their contributions to the US war effort.

Five of the 55 WASP still living at the time were in attendance. The youngest in Sweetwater that weekend was 95 years old.

From more than 20,000 candidates, 1,074 women flew for the US Army Air Forces from September 1942 through December 1944. They ferried and flight-tested aircraft, towed gunnery targets, and transported equipment and personnel.

Their duties enabled men to serve in active combat roles.

Unlike their male counterparts, each WASP personally paid for her own transportation costs to training sites, for her dress uniforms there, and for room and board while being instructed.

When a WASP died in service to country, families were financially responsible for the return home of their daughters' remains, unlike their male counterparts who made the ultimate sacrifice.

Not until 1977 were WASP finally given "veteran" status and made eligible for military benefits.

Even then, the legislation was vigorously opposed by the Veterans Administration, the American Legion, and the Veterans of Foreign Wars.

In fact, for more than 30 years following the conclusion of World War II, all WASP records were sealed by the government and the women were told to keep quiet about their wartime experience.

But during the war, their involvement was news.

On Monday, April 24, 1944, a front-page story in *The Bryan Daily Eagle* announced that a "cadre" of 14 WASP had begun the Instrumentation Pilot Instructors' Course at the AAF "University of Instrument Flying" at Bryan Field.

The women arrived from installations around the country: Merced, California; Las Vegas, Nevada; Lawrenceville, Illinois; and Stuttgart, Arkansas, as well as Texas bases in Sweetwater, Pecos, and San Antonio.

The story cited the women's status as civilian pilots but emphasized they would be receiving the same training as Army Air Forces officers.

Later during World War II, other WASP came through Bryan Field for training, but, according to the official WASP archives at Texas Women's University in Denton, only two were permanently stationed at the base.

Suzanne DeLano and Joan Michaels reported for duty at Bryan Army Air Field on August 10, 1944. After completing the Instrument Instructor course, they remained at the base until the WASP program was deactivated in the days before Christmas that same year.

General H. H. "Hap" Arnold, the head of the US Army Air Forces, begrudgingly ended the WASP's military involvement.

Suzanne DeLano. Courtesy of Texas Woman's University, Woman's Collection.

Joan Michaels. Courtesy of Texas Woman's University, Woman's Collection.

At the outset of World War II, Arnold opposed the idea of women serving as pilots in the Army.

Eventually he acquiesced, principally because men were needed for overseas duty.

Still, while women were allowed to fly, Arnold rejected the idea they be commissioned into the Women's Army Auxiliary Corps.

Eventually, he changed his mind about that.

Suzanne DeLano and Joan Michaels discovered their love of flying in very different ways.

DeLano was born in New York City and raised in France, a child of privilege and the granddaughter of William E. Upjohn, founder of the Upjohn pharmaceutical company.

She loved horses and upon her return to the United States intended to be a veterinarian, but a broken ankle, suffered while taking a bad spill while riding, changed her plans.

While recuperating, "I was restless, getting on my mother's nerves," Suzanne DeLano Parish said in later years, "so she suggested I take flying lessons.

"I loved it so much that flying became my passion."

DeLano earned her WASP wings in Sweetwater, where all WASP went through the same seven-month basic training program that the Army Air Forces' male cadets experienced elsewhere.

She was assigned to Bryan Field as a "test pilot." DeLano flew with men returning from oversees combat duty who needed instrument flying time. In addition, she flight-tested repaired planes to ensure they would be safe . . . for men to fly.

After the war, DeLano married Preston Parish, a Marine Air Corps veteran. The couple settled in Kalamazoo, Michigan, where Upjohn's corporate headquarters were located. Desperately wanting to continue to fly, Suzanne was rejected at every turn in her efforts to become a pilot for an aviation company or airline.

She even lobbied her uncle, John Gilmore, for a job as a corporate pilot for the family's pharmaceutical business.

Gilmore, as president of the company, said no, too.

Suzanne and her husband eventually established the Kalamazoo Aviation History Museum in 1977, known today as the Air Zoo. More importantly, they bought a partial interest in an airplane, and Suzanne resumed her flying career.

For more than a quarter century, she dazzled air-show audiences around the country flying her pink Curtiss P-40 Warhawk.

Joan Michaels' father, Marion Grevenberg, flew pursuit planes in World War I. A between-wars flight with his daughter over the Statue of Liberty triggered her love of aviation.

By the time the WASP program was established, Joan, from Virginia, was ready to follow in her father's footsteps. With her pilot's license in hand and ample flight time under her belt, she easily qualified to become an aviatrix.

No one was more proud of Joan than her father, by that time a lieutenant colonel in the wartime Army Air Forces. At her Avenger Field graduation ceremony, Grevenberg presented his daughter her silver wings.

Joan Michaels and Suzanne DeLano were classmates in Sweetwater. Both reported for duty at Bryan Field in the late summer of 1944.

Both knew, upon their arrival, their time in service to country would be short.

Witnessing the WASP's stateside contributions to the war effort, Hap Arnold's opinion of women serving in his Army Air Forces changed dramatically. He became a supporter of a plan to commission WASP pilots in the Army.

But an effort to gain Congressional approval for the measure fell short of passage.

Frustrated by the lawmakers' decision, Arnold announced on June 26, 1944, that the WASP program would be discontinued at year's end.

That December, just days before the WASP would be dismissed, Arnold spoke at Avenger Field.

"The WASP has completed its mission. Their job has been successful. But as is usual in war, the cost has been heavy. Thirty-eight WASP have died while helping their country move toward the moment of final victory. The Air Force will long remember their service and their final sacrifice."

Sixty-five years later, in 2009, Barak Obama signed a presidential order presenting each and every WASP, living or deceased, with a Congressional Gold Medal, the nation's highest honor for civilians.

Among the 300 or so surviving WASP honored by presidential decree were Suzanne DeLano Parish and Joan Michaels Lemley.

Parish died in 2010 and Lemley in 2015.

Another WASP to receive the Congressional Gold Medal was Bryan native Catherine Parker Chatham.

Bryan native and WASP Catherine Parker Chatham. Courtesy of Texas Woman's University, Woman's Collection.

After earning her wings at Avenger Field, Parker was stationed at Marana Airfield in Tucson, Arizona. After the war, she returned to Bryan, married Roland Chatham, and helped grow his photography business by flying him for aerial assignments.

In *The Eagle* series "Brazos Valley Veterans," Bryan attorney Bill Youngkin interviewed Chatham, who died in 2016, about her time as a WASP.

"I loved to fly," she told Youngkin. "My first solo was an exhilarating experience.

"I never got tired of looking down at the world I came from."

Nancy Currie-Gregg

Just as the Tuskegee Airmen paved the way for future generations of African Americans, so, too, did the Women Airforce Service Pilots set precedents and inspire dreams enabling others to follow in their slipstream.

Dr. Nancy Currie-Gregg is a NASA astronaut. She flew four times on the Space Shuttle. Before that, she was a military helicopter pilot, serving more than 20 years in the US Army and retiring at the rank of colonel.

Today, she teaches in the Texas A&M Industrial and Systems Engineering Department as a professor of the practice.

In Service to Country

"Our nation owes the Women Airforce Service Pilots an enormous debt of gratitude for their contributions during World War II. They were willing and capable aviators and in almost every way possible, from the training they received to the duties they performed, they proved themselves equal to their male counterparts.

"As an Army aviator myself, and an astronaut, I feel a special kinship with the WASP because they helped open doors through which I was able to pass. But their role in history goes beyond merely 'breaking barriers.'

"People sometimes ask me what it's like to be a 'pioneer.' I tell them I don't use that word to describe myself. In both my military service and exploration of space, I was simply doing my job. And fortunately, I was always provided the tools, support, and guidance to do that job to the best of my ability.

"As the saying goes, 'We've come a long way.'

"If you want to talk about a real pioneer, look no further than Cornelia Fort, a WASP from Nashville, Tennessee.

"Cornelia was a civilian instructor pilot at Pearl Harbor in Hawaii when on December 7, 1941, while she was teaching takeoffs and landings to a student, she inadvertently ran into the first wave of Japanese aircraft in their attack on the US Naval base located on the island. After hurriedly landing her aircraft ahead of the invasion, her plane was strafed by Japanese gunnery fire. She and her student managed to run to cover and survive.

Nancy Currie-Gregg *spent the majority of her military and government careers supporting NASA's human spaceflight programs and projects. A member of NASA's Astronaut Corps from 1990 to 2005, Currie-Gregg accrued 1,000 hours in space as a mission specialist on four Space Shuttle flights. A Master Army Aviator, she also logged over 4,000 flying hours in a variety of rotary-wing and fixed-wing aircraft, retiring at the rank of colonel. Following her astronaut career, Currie-Gregg served in a variety of senior engineering and safety positions at NASA. She joined the faculty at Texas A&M University in 2017 as a professor in the College of Engineering's Industrial Engineering Department. Currie-Gregg is a member of both the Women in Aviation International Hall of Fame and the Army Aviation Hall of Fame.*

Courtesy of the National Aeronautics and Space Administration.

“Many of the seamen she knew at Pearl Harbor were not as fortunate that day. More than 2,400 American service personnel died in the attack.

“Fifteen months later on March 21, 1943, Cornelia was putting her flying skills to use ferrying aircraft for the US Army Air Forces as a WASP. While on a mission to Texas from her home base in Long Beach, California, the left wing of her plane accidentally clipped the landing gear of her flight officer’s plane just above her. He recovered and eventually landed safely. Cornelia fell into an irreversible dive and crashed into Mulberry Canyon, near Abilene.

“Cornelia was the first WASP to die for her country. Her parents had to collect her remains and make arrangements for their daughter’s burial.

“That was just one of the unjust challenges which the WASP faced in their service to country. They were denied commissions into the Army, told to keep silent about their activities after the war, and prevented from receiving veteran benefits for decades.

“Only in the last 10 years are the WASP finally receiving what should have always been rightfully theirs.

“In 2016, WASP Elaine Danforth Harmon was buried at Arlington National Cemetery. While she was the first WASP to receive that honor, it took almost 180,000 petition signatures for the United States Congress to finally avail the hallowed ground of Arlington to brave women like Elaine.

“The spirit of Cornelia and Elaine; of Suzanne DeLano Parrish and Joan Michaels Lemley who were stationed as WASP at Bryan Army Air Field, lives on in the hearts of women like me and in places like today’s RELLIS Campus.

“Almost all now are gone, but none should ever be forgotten.”

Program cover from the 1943 Texas A&M vs. Bryan Field football game. Courtesy of Cushing Memorial Library & Archives, Texas A&M University.

CHAPTER 8
Service Teams

> ***"Stimulated by the presence of several new candidates previously unable to turn out for daily practice, and a stepping up of the defensive workouts, the Bryan Field football team is pointing to their game with Texas A. and M. at College Station on Saturday, September 25th."***

The story, which appeared on the front page of the September 24, 1943, edition of *The Hearne Democrat,* went on to report that though the Bryan Field squad was "small in number," it was also "spirited and rugged."

Just not rugged enough.

Jimbo Fisher would have been proud of the Aggies' performance which opened the 1943 season. A&M routed Bryan Field 48-6.

In fact, then coach Homer Norton's Aggies built on that win to go undefeated heading into the year's regular-season finale against Texas.

The Aggies lost that game 27-13, then lost in the Orange Bowl to LSU 19-14, but still finished a surprising 7-2-1 on the year.

That was a remarkable achievement, almost on par with Texas A&M's national-championship season under Norton in 1939.

A&M entered its 1943 campaign losing 77 of 84 players to military duty. Many of those on the squad Norton was able to field had never played organized football.

And, with an average age of just 17, the 1943 Aggies became known as the "Kiddie Korps."

In a 1971 *Sports Illustrated* article entitled, "When Football Went to War," writer Charles Einstein—no kin to the famed theoretical physicist but half-brother to actor and comedian Albert Brooks, whose real name is, indeed, "Albert Einstein"—illuminated the college football landscape during World War II.

"The wartime college game in America was played at two levels," wrote Einstein, "one a kind of enforced deemphasis among the colleges and universities and the other, far closer to the collegiate game as it had been known, among teams representing various Army, Navy, and Marine installations."

A look at 1943's final Associated Press football poll is revealing.

Notre Dame won the national championship that year.

The Iowa Pre-Flight Seahawks, representing the US Navy's pre-flight school at the University of Iowa in Iowa City, finished second with a 9-1 record.

Also ranked in the AP's season-ending top 10: Great Lakes Navy, Del Monte Pre-Flight, and March Field.

The Bryan Field football program, coached by the base's physical training department head, Lieutenant Roy Johnson, was several notches below the elite service powerhouses.

The team's original 1943 schedule included just five games: the matchup against Texas A&M, a home and away series against the Randolph Field Ramblers, an away contest at Blackland Army Flying School in Waco, and a season-ending matchup versus Southwestern University in Georgetown, Texas.

The game against Southwestern was scrapped after the lopsided loss to A&M. Southwestern was a football powerhouse back in the day, winning its first five games in 1943 to climb to Number 13 in the AP poll.

Instead, Bryan Field ended its year against Camp Hearne, a POW internment post and site of a Bryan Field auxiliary airstrip, beating the Warriors 6-0.

Throughout the game story of that matchup, in the November 15, 1943, issue of *The Bryan Daily Eagle*, no mention is made of a nickname for the Bryan Field team.

BAAF Base Commander Colonel Joseph Duckworth (*left in photo*) with the Bryan Field football coaching staff. Courtesy of Cushing Memorial Library & Archives, Texas A&M University.

Team photo of Bryan Army Air Field football team. Courtesy of *The Eagle* newspaper.

However, kudos were given to the team's lineman Ralph O'Hair for his showing at end. In an era when players went "both ways," the story reports that O'Hair "stopped several Hearne drives with his hard tackling, and grabbed several Bryan passes."

As a flight navigator, Lieutenant O'Hair also sat in the backseat behind base commander Joseph Duckworth on history's first intentional flight into a hurricane during the summer of 1943.

Sadly, no one thought to call O'Hair and his teammates "The Hurricane."

As a result of base and local community segregation, Bryan Field showcased a second football team in 1943.

The 325th Aviation Squadron team, comprised exclusively of black servicemen stationed at the installation, played "home" games at Bryan's all-black Kemp High School.

Against Prairie View College in a home-and-home series on back-to-back Saturdays in November 1943, the 325th airmen lost twice. *The Bryan Daily Eagle* reported, "The Prairie View eleven (was) largely composed of college stars now in the service and registered in the Special Training Unit at the college."

Football was, by no means, the only game at Bryan Field, nor at other military installations across the country. Sports boosted morale, fostered teamwork, and instilled a competitive spirit.

Sports stories frequently rated front-page placement in *The Panel*, the Bryan Field base newspaper. In the August 3, 1945, edition, a team photo of the Squadron B softball team proclaimed them to be "first half champions."

A month later, a *Panel* headline read, "Tennis Champ To Be Picked In Singles Tourney This Month."

According to the story, "valuable prizes" were at stake, and "a limited number of rackets (were) available at the Physical Training office."

Pilots from several European countries trained at Bryan Air Force Base during the Korean War and afterwards. So it is not surprising the base fielded a soccer team, too.

Captain Dionysius Roxs was liaison officer for jet pilot trainees from the Netherlands. Roxs was well known in the Bryan community, popular for his civic and garden-club talks.

It was his idea to start a Bryan Air Force Base soccer team in 1953.

"When I came to America, I didn't like football or baseball," Roxs told a reporter from *The Bryan Daily Eagle*, "because I didn't understand the games.

"Americans are the same about soccer," he noted.

Hoping to infuse a love of soccer in locals, the former Dutch-playing standout and his Bryan Air Force Base team competed in the Texas International Soccer League. Foes included Texas A&M, the University of Texas, and Allen Academy, then a military school in Bryan.

A drive around today's RELLIS Campus offers no indication of where Roxs' team might have practiced and played. Remarkably though, the fencing and backstop comprising the installation's baseball and softball field has stood the test of time.

More than 500 big-leaguers served in the military during World War II. Remarkably, only two died.

Those two were Elmer Gedeon and Harry O'Neill, and neither man was anything close to being a star. Gedeon played five games for the Washington Senators. O'Neill caught two innings for the Philadelphia Athletics.

A website called Baseball's Greatest Sacrifice pays tribute to men like Gedeon and O'Neill, players who made the "ultimate sacrifice" in service to country.

"On August 26, 1955, the Bryan Air Force Base baseball team was traveling by bus to a tournament at Barksdale Air Force Base in Shreveport, Louisiana," the website reports. "About three miles from Cushing, Texas, the bus blew a tire and plunged over a 30-foot embankment into a dry creek.

"The injured managed to crawl out windows or were helped out by rescuers."

Two enlisted men, however, died in the accident: Airman First Class Lloyd Buresh, an infielder from Karlin, Missouri, and Airman First Class James Kirkpatrick of Buff City, Tennessee, driver of the bus.

According to Department of Defense figures released in 1993, 33,686 Americans were killed in battle during the Korean War. Another 2,830 Americans lost their lives in Korea in noncombat activities.

Back home, 17,730 Department of Defense deaths were recorded during American involvement in the Korean conflict. That number includes Buresh and Kirkpatrick.

Their funerals took place, as did so many others for men who perished preparing for war at both Bryan Field and Bryan Air Force Base, at the post's chapel, which still stands today.

Old baseball and softball field backstop at the RELLIS Campus. Photo by author.

Special Service Section

On the athletic fields of military endeavor, pursuits like football and baseball offered an enjoyable and purposeful pastime for service men stationed at places like Bryan Army Air Field. But, sports weren't the only means by which the military sought to keep soldiers' spirits high.

Special Service was the "entertainment" branch of the US military. The War Department launched the unit in the summer of 1940, nearly a year and a half before America's entry into the Second World War.

Special Service opportunities were plentiful on post, as outlined in the "history" of Bryan Field assembled in 1944. That document provided detailed descriptions of duties and responsibilities at the base, including those afforded by Special Service.

"It's a Heck of a Mess"

The Special Service section at Bryan Field was activated on January 3, 1943, by appointment of Second Lieutenant J. M. O'Leary as Special Service Officer. The Special Service Officer was detailed with the following duties: Officers Club, Library, Theater, Insurance, War Bonds, Army Emergency Relief, Band Commander, and School and/or Education Officer, other than technical school.

On March 19, the Field's first radio program, presented over WTAW at Texas A&M College, was offered. The program was a 15-minute production known as "Bryan Field on the Air" and continued as a weekly program until February 25, 1944, at which time it was changed to a 30-minute program and renamed "The KIWI Jamboree." Plans are at the present time under way to make this a remote broadcast, presenting it at the Post Theater as a stage show at the same time.

On April 25 the Field received its first Blue Circuit USO show, which was presented in the Recreation Building to an enthusiastic crowd. These shows continued to put in appearances at the rate of about two a month until July when the Special Service Department succeeded in having the Field placed on the White Circuit, the first show being presented at the Field on July 31.

Bryan Field's first soldier show, titled "It's A Heck of a Mess," composed of original music, skits, and verse, was represented on the Field on May 11, 1943, and was an outstanding success and a worthy send-off for the soldier show program, which has been functioning regularly from that time to the present. This show was also presented in the local community and was well received by a full house. After all expenses were paid, a tidy profit was donated to the Welfare and Recreation fund.

During April 1943, the Special Service Department started handling the sale of newspapers on the Post, after trying unsuccessfully for at least 30 days previously to have them handled either direct by the Post Exchange or by civilian newsboys. As a result of the profit made on the newspapers, it was possible to begin the printing of a camp newspaper, the first issue of which came out under a date line of May 29, 1943, and was later named "The Panel." For the first three months of its existence, this was a four-page tabloid-size sheet, with practically no art work, but in September, through the assistance of the Post Exchange, the paper was increased to eight pages and included both local pictures and art work and newspaper service pictures of world-wide interest.

The arrival of the 420th AAF Band during the month of March, and the immediate formation of a dance orchestra from band personnel, was the starting point for entertainment activities on the Post. The first Post dance was held in May and dances have continued at the rate of at least one a month since that time. The largest difficulty encountered in these dances was procuring enough girls for the number of men involved. For the first few dances the Young Women's Service

Organization of Bryan cooperated in bringing out a large percentage of their membership, and this continued in a fairly satisfactory manner until the USO took over and absorbed the organization.

The Field experienced considerable difficulty in the lack of facilities for the control of venereal disease. The venereal rate on this Field, month after month, was among the highest in the Training Center. Through a concentrated course of education, instruction, and supervision on the Field, and a gradual improvement in local civilian cooperation, the rate was very slowly decreased.

The arrival of a colored squadron on the Field brought up an immediate recreational and morale problem, which is still in the process of being solved. The first efforts to relieve the situation were semi-monthly dances and stag parties held on the Field in the colored area. The establishment of a colored Service Club has effectively prevented any possible unpleasantness along racial lines. The colored section at the Post Theater and Recreation Hall are designated only by the squadron number. No definite discriminations are made. Definite results in the past six months from these combined efforts are reflected in the monthly lowering of the venereal disease rate in the squadron.

Six bowling alleys were purchased during March 1943 through the medium of the Post facility. The alleys opened at an inopportune time facing the hottest weather, but the Bowling Alley has never failed to meet all obligations. The main difficulty in the operation of the Bowling Alley rested in the procurement of pin boys, but, after receiving the authority quoted, colored soldiers were used with satisfactory results.

Bill Lay kneels beside the RELLIS Campus plaque honoring Aggies who attended their first year of college at The Annex. Photo by author.

CHAPTER 9
Remembering the Annex

Ione Lay looked proudly at her eldest son, Billy. She nodded approvingly as she prepared to say goodbye.

Billy was set to begin his first year at the A&M College of Texas. Thanks to his parents' encouragement, he had chosen to continue his education, the first in his family to attend college.

Tears began to fill Ione's eyes. Not wanting to create a scene in front of her son, she gave Billy one last hug, turned, and got into the family car.

Bill Lay spent more than 20 years as the director of admissions for Texas A&M University. Enjoying retirement, Lay and his wife, Mary Jo, still call the Bryan-College Station area home.

Lay's time in Aggieland began in the late summer of 1949. Bill still remembers his mother's sniffles as she left him behind at The Annex, the Bryan Army Air Field home to A&M freshmen cadets from 1946 to 1950.

"She later told me she was crying because she thought it was the most barren place she had ever seen," Lay says today.

Airfield Road now marks the main entrance to the new RELLIS Campus. Along that thoroughfare, just past Bryan Road and the turn-off to the Blinn College Schwartz Classroom Building, sits a marker, a tribute to the Classes of 1950, 1951, 1952, and 1953, all of which began their A&M experience at The Annex.

Usage of the Bryan Field complex helped then A&M President Gibb Gilchrist address two pressing issues in the immediate aftermath of World War II.

The availability of the facility gave his college the ability to handle the postwar surge of students wanting to attend A&M. Those numbers included both high school graduates and military veterans beginning or continuing their education under the GI Bill.

More than 20,000 A&M cadets served their country during World War II. More than 14,000 of those were officers. Twenty-nine were generals. All spoke highly of their college experience and proved to be good ambassadors for the college.

Dormitory space on A&M's main campus after World War II was woefully inadequate for the dramatic increase in student numbers.

Thus, new Aggie cadets would spend their first, or "fish," year of school living in the barracks of the recently deactivated Army Air Forces' installation about 10 miles north of the main campus.

Because of that distance, it was determined fish would both live and learn at what came to be called The Annex.

"There were about 1,300 of us out there," Lay says of his freshman class. "The barracks were thin-shelled, tarpaper shacks. Not exactly a picturesque setting."

Members of the Texas A&M College Fish Band at The Annex in 1949. Billy Lay is third from right, second row. Courtesy of Bill Lay.

A&M faculty commuted to The Annex to teach classes. At the time, the first-year curricula was structured the same for virtually all students.

Billy Lay joined the Fish Band. The Fish Drill Team, formed at The Annex in 1946, practiced long hours on the site, eventually becoming world-famous for its precision marching routines.

In addition to helping A&M solve its housing shortage, The Annex also addressed another of Gilchrist's concerns.

As with many military schools, upperclassmen among A&M's Corps of Cadets saw it as their sworn duty to "indoctrinate" first-year students. Newly incarcerated prison inmates have long been called "fish," swimming upstream into the harsh environment of a penal institution.

Within the Corps, the term was intended to be demeaning, like "doolies," "plebes," or "rats" elsewhere.

Other forms of hazing at A&M, meant to toughen newcomers physically and psychologically, were far more tortuous than merely being called a "fish."

When The Annex was opened in the fall of 1946, the incoming freshmen class included a large contingent of World War II veterans. Their involvement in the Corps was not mandatory.

Hazing of their ranks by younger upperclassmen lacking in actual combat experience would not have been a good idea.

And so, true freshmen like Billy Lay got a slight reprieve.

"As challenging as conditions were at The Annex," Lay chuckles, "I don't think I would have traded my year there for a year of hazing on the main campus.

"Which is not to say a little hazing didn't take place anyway," he adds.

Fish were bussed from The Annex to Kyle Field for Aggie football games. A time-honored tradition required first-year cadets to know the names and hometowns of all players.

Under duress, that critical information sometimes slipped the mind of a harrowed fish.

"Punishment" was swift.

While game-day could be a taxing experience for freshmen like Lay, he says living at The Annex had an important upside.

"It bonded us," says Lay. "I still have friendships that I established there . . . and that was a long time ago.

"All of us who lived out there are the 'Class of '53.'"

Lay actually graduated in 1954, and, in an ironic twist of fate, he returned to The Annex site a year later.

"After going through the ROTC program at A&M, I was eligible to become a second lieutenant in the Air Force," Lay says. "But at the time, there were only a limited number of spots available for commissioned officers.

"I could have entered the service as an airman first class, but I chose to wait. I spent the next year teaching back home in Pasadena.

"The following year, I was called to active duty, commissioned as a second lieutenant, and of all the places they could have sent me, I wound up being stationed at Bryan Air Force Base in 1955."

When Bryan Field was reactivated for the Korean War, the name was changed. The Army Air Forces became the US Air Force in 1947.

Aggie fish returned to campus for the fall semester of 1950.

Lay's assignment at Bryan Air Force Base foreshadowed his post-military career.

"I was an administrative officer, responsible for maintaining the records of the pilots who came through the school there," Lay says. "Sort of like being the registrar at a university."

And, just as he would experience as Texas A&M's director of admissions, not every young Air Force officer was cut out for success.

"That was the beginning of my real education in life," Lay says. "Most of the young pilots I dealt with didn't like to see me because that meant they had some failing which might lead to them washing out of the program."

Lay served at Bryan Air Force Base until it closed in 1958. While there he met and married Mary Jo. They've been together for 62 years.

Lay's next tour of duty was in England. He left the Air Force in the summer of 1962.

Bill Lay has a great appreciation for the history of the RELLIS Campus. He personally experienced two of its most compelling chapters. But Lay also has, perhaps more than many, an understanding of what RELLIS will be in the future.

"I like the idea of 'pooling the resources' of a variety of academic institutions," Lay says of RELLIS's "Academic Alliance" involving Blinn College and the non-flagship institutions of the Texas A&M University System. "This should allow us to do some things that we wouldn't be able to do otherwise.

"I think it's important," Lay adds, "that the students who attend school where I spent my *freshman year of college understand that RELLIS has a vibrant legacy, both in serving our country and helping Texas A&M achieve its academic goals."

Photo of "fish" on a barracks bunk at The Annex. Courtesy of Cushing Memorial Library & Archives, Texas A&M University.

Jack Fritts' Aggie Muster Speech

Aggie Muster is a time-honored A&M tradition that celebrates those core values and the spirit of camaraderie around which the school was conceived. At Muster celebrations around the world every April 21, Aggies who have died, specifically those in the past year, are remembered and honored.

Jerry Cooper is the former editor of *Texas Aggie* magazine, the Association of Former Students alumni publication. A prolific contributor to the Texas A&M University Press, Cooper's most recent work is *"HERE": The Muster Speeches at Texas A&M University.*

Jack Fritts, A&M Class of 1953, presented the keynote speech at the main campus Muster ceremony in 1993. This is an excerpt from Fritts' speech contained in Cooper's outstanding book.

"We Dared Not Go 'Upstream'"

"After World War II, many Aggies came back to A&M to finish their education, which had been disrupted by the global conflict. So many in fact that the university was overflowing. No major construction had been done the previous four years, so the facilities were stretched to the breaking point.

"In 1946, the administration decided to send the freshman class for the next four years to the old Brian Army Air (Field), or as the elaborate brochures described it—The Texas A&M College Annex. A 'unique learning experience' is what they said, 'where there are plenty of dormitories, classrooms, and drill fields!' Each Aggie in the Classes of '50, '51, '52, and '53 spent two semesters living with 19 other men in army barracks, sleeping in bunk beds and with your 'old lady,' or bunkmate, sharing a small table for a desk. We had to go to another barracks to shower, shave, and use the toilet facilities. We drilled on the airstrip and dined in a real old-army mess hall and our favorite recreation was avoiding contact with 'wetheads' (sophomores). The headquarters barracks was next to mine and the bugle stand was at the headquarters. That bugler was drowned out nearly every morning at 6:00 by those who would have preferred to sleep in. And talking about "wetheads," my side of the first few conversations I had with them went something like this: "'My first name is what?', 'What is a whip out?', 'I'm supposed to hit a what?', 'I'm supposed to call you, "Mister"?', 'What do you mean, I can't say, "I don't know"?', 'What in the world is a "bullring"?', 'You mean I have to stand up for the whole game?'".

"When we wanted to go somewhere on a weekend, we got out on Highway 21 and hitchhiked.

"Very few fish had cars. Buses were too expensive. I remember the Aggie lines we used for hitchhiking from one city to another when we were ready to go somewhere. We went to a specific location in town and took our place in line and waited to work our way up to the front. We dared not go 'upstream' or cut in front of the line, but we were welcomed to go downstream if we wished. Many times I spent hours hung up in Caldwell or Hempstead or Navasota or Hearne trying to go to Dallas or Austin or any of the other major cities. Despite all that adversity, those four classes have consistently been among the leaders in contributions of time and money to the Association of Former Students and to this university."

Jack Fritts *earned a bachelor's degree in animal husbandry from Texas A&M. He was president of the Association of Former Students in 1982 and a key figure in initiating plans for construction of the Clayton W. Williams Jr. Alumni Center. He also served as chairman of the building committee that had gifts and pledges in hand to pay for the $7 million structure on the day it opened in 1987. Fritts originated the candlelight ceremony that is now an integral part of Aggie Muster and was named a Distinguished Alumnus of Texas A&M in 1987.*

Courtesy of Texas A&M Association of Former Students.

Buzz Aldrin at the RELLIS Campus in the spring of 2018. Photo by author.

CHAPTER 10
Second Man

The second man disembarking the transport shuttle at the RELLIS Campus Center for Infrastructure Renewal building shifted gingerly from the front passenger seat of the van. Extending his right foot slowly toward the ground, a red-and-white striped sock revealed itself, matching the stars-and-stripes tie he sported with his dark blue suit. Carefully, but without assistance, the visitor finally planted himself on solid ground.

Buzz Aldrin looked at his surroundings and smiled.

With just a little imagination, this seemingly inconsequential scene much resembled Aldrin's descent down the landing leg of the Lunar Excursion Module . . . nearly 50 years ago.

From that celestial vantage point, he offered this description to the hundreds of millions of earthbound television viewers watching back home: "A beautiful view, magnificent desolation."

On July 20, 1969, Aldrin and fellow astronaut Neil Armstrong became the first humans to walk on the moon.

Aldrin's May 14, 2018, visit to the Bryan-College Station area marked another milestone in the life of the 88-year-old former Apollo 11 astronaut.

At the RELLIS Campus site in 1952, Aldrin went through advanced pilot training while a 22-year old second lieutenant stationed at Bryan Air Force Base.

Asked when he'd last seen the place, Aldrin chuckled.

"I've been thinking about that," he said with a smile.

After a pause as he continued to think, Aldrin finally offered, "In my mind, many times."

Aldrin's recent stop on the RELLIS Campus was part of a fact-finding mission. In addition to being a retired Air Force colonel and holder of a PhD degree from MIT, Aldrin recently added yet another title to his distinguished resume.

He is chancellor of the International Space University.

Aldrin is seeking to broaden the horizons of the interdisciplinary educational and research institute he now heads. Founded in 1987 at MIT, the International Space University today is located in the suburbs of Strasbourg, France.

"As chancellor," Aldrin said, "hopefully I get to say something about the predominant influence of the US experience into the international space program. Therefore, a good bit of it should be here in the United States."

Perhaps even in the Lone Star State.

"In looking at options, Texas A&M is a logical place to do this."

What "this" might entail is why Aldrin, while here, met with officials from the Texas A&M University System. He believes the proximity of both the A&M flagship campus and the RELLIS site to the Johnson

Space Center in Houston makes the A&M System a candidate to host an extension of the International Space University.

Buzz—and that's been his legal name for 30 years—is well known for imploring mankind to "Get Your Ass To Mars" and doing all he can to ensure that happens.

As for what happened to him during his three-month stop as a fighter-pilot-in-training at Bryan Air Force Base more than 65 years ago, Aldrin has two very vivid recollections.

One may have been, to that point, the proudest moment of his already distinguished young life. The other nearly cut that life short.

"I give talks every so often and I see a picture of my father and me in a T-33," Aldrin said, "and he's sitting in the back and I'm sitting in the front."

The photo was taken at Bryan Air Force Base.

"I have to tell my audiences, 'I had just gotten my wings. You don't think they were going to let me take up an aviation pioneer in the back seat?

"'This was just a photo op.'"

In his memoir, *Return to Earth*, published in 1973, Aldrin wrote that his father did get a flight that day with one of Bryan Air Force Base's more experienced instructors.

Edwin Eugene Aldrin Sr., Buzz's father, was a military aviator too. Both father and son rose to the rank of colonel and both obtained doctoral degrees from MIT. E. E. Aldrin worked as an executive with Standard Oil of New Jersey, and it was in the company's famed Lockheed Vega NC 106N that Buzz took his first flight, out of Newark Airport, at the age of two.

"I got a little sick," Buzz admitted.

Aldrin's father was well known and well regarded in the aviation world. He was well acquainted with some of the biggest names in flying.

Emulating one of his father's friends nearly proved fatal for Aldrin while learning to become a fighter pilot at Bryan Air Force Base.

"Jimmy Doolittle was famous for making an 'outside loop,'" Aldrin said in explaining the episode in which he nearly "bought the farm," although common usage of that phrase to indicate a fatal crash seems to have begun after Aldrin's time at Bryan Air Force Base.

"I learned that you could make an 'Immelmann,'" a looping flight maneuver, "and on the top you could do a 'double Immelmann.'"

Aldrin attempted this maneuver in the skies over Bryan and College Station flying a single-propeller T-28 trainer.

"You got to get going pretty fast," Aldrin explained, "and then you've got to pull back on the stick. And this is what I did in a T-28 . . ."

As he spoke these words, Aldrin closed his eyes.

"And that's the last I remembered."

Extreme g-forces caused Aldrin to momentarily lose consciousness, a condition pilots call a "gray out."

"I'm asleep. I'm out. Next thing I know," Aldrin pointed straight down with his flattened hand," I'm heading for Texas."

When he woke, he noticed, "I've got something in this hand and something in this hand," referring to the control wheel of his aircraft. "And I had the presence of mind to ease back on both of them," averting disaster in the nick of time.

In *Return to Earth*, Aldrin wrote that he was more puzzled than alarmed at his circumstances. In person, he added, "You think you'd learn from that."

He didn't, particularly when given an F-86 to fly while serving as a gunnery instructor at Nellis Air Force Base near Las Vegas after the Korean War.

"That was too much of a temptation. I'm going to do that 'double Immelmann.'

"So, I get up pretty high and dive down and yank back on the stick . . .

" . . . something snaps in my neck."

In telling the story, a pained look crossed his face.

"And, so I ease over like this." This time, he raised his hand to trace a gentle downward slope. "I'm thinking, 'If I can ever get this on the ground they're going to have to come with a crane to lift me up.'"

Which, one supposes, is the price to be paid for having "the right stuff."

Or at least trying to find out if you do.

One can't spend an hour with Buzz Aldrin without hearing a little about his time on the moon.

As he shifted to the topic, he posed a culturally profound question. Or at least one that seemed to suggest historical importance.

"What is the significance of Americans being the first?"

Is there anyone on earth more qualified to answer that?

"Well, we ended up getting very practical."

Upon hearing this, thoughts immediately rocket toward Mars. Aldrin believes we should go there. He collectively chides us for not having already made the trip.

Did we, as a species whose DNA drives us toward exploration, fall victim to "practicality?"

It turns out Aldrin wasn't offering his interviewer a broad view of our place and responsibilities in the cosmos. Rather—and somewhat anticlimactically—he was merely reflecting on what he calls the "symbology" of Apollo 11.

Still, that's good stuff.

"Neil and I decided that our call sign would be *Eagle*," the name given the lunar lander in which he and fellow astronaut Armstrong descended upon the moon.

The matter-of-fact way in which Aldrin described one of the most significant events in human history suggests he's told this part of that story a time or two.

"'Houston, Tranquility Base. The *Eagle* has landed.'

"'Tranquility Base?' Where did that come from?"

Aldrin explained that he and his crew mates decided once *Eagle* was on the moon, an exploratory "outpost" would have been established.

"Neil had the honor of doing all these 'pronouncements,' Aldrin added. "First symbolic person. . . .

". . . 'Small step for man.'

". . . 'Giant leap for mankind.'"

Hearing Armstrong's famous words spoken by Aldrin is more than a little surreal. The record suggests there was friction between the two men regarding who would own the privilege of being the first person to set foot upon the moon.

In *Return to Earth*, Aldrin writes that his father was more insistent than he that Buzz should be the "first man." It's clear in the book—and in speaking with Aldrin in person—that he has a great deal of respect and affection for his father, the man who shaped his thinking and his career.

Spending time with Buzz, it's pretty obvious he wanted to make his father proud.

"To get technical about it, I had the first words," Aldrin stated for the record during his RELLIS Campus interview. Uttering this pronouncement, a somewhat mischievous grin crossed his face.

"When we touched down, there was a little light that comes on and when it comes on, I say, 'Contact light. Engines stop.'

"And then there were a few other things. So, *those* were the first words."

A paperback edition of another of Aldrin's books, *No Dream Is Too High*, was recently released. Aldrin dedicates the book to "dreamers like me," including Stephen Hawking; John Houbolt, who devised the ingenious plan to ferry a disposable lunar landing craft to the moon; and fellow astronauts Charles Bassett and Ed White.

Bassett was Aldrin's backyard neighbor in the Houston suburb of Nassau Bay, where many of NASA's astronauts lived in the mid-1960s. Preparing for his *Gemini 9* flight, Bassett died in a T-38 plane crash in St. Louis.

Bassett's death in 1966, along with crew mate Elliot See, moved Aldrin up a spot in the Gemini crew rotation. Aldrin eventually flew on the final Gemini mission. Had he missed out on the Gemini program, he would have been an unlikely choice for Apollo 11.

Like Aldrin, Charlie Bassett was a student pilot at Bryan Air Force Base.

So was Ted Freeman, astronaut classmate to Aldrin and Bassett. Freeman also died in a T-38 accident before flying into space.

Second Lieutenant Edwin Eugene Aldrin Jr., 22, in the cockpit of a T-33 *Shooting Star* at Bryan Air Force Base. Courtesy of US Air Force.

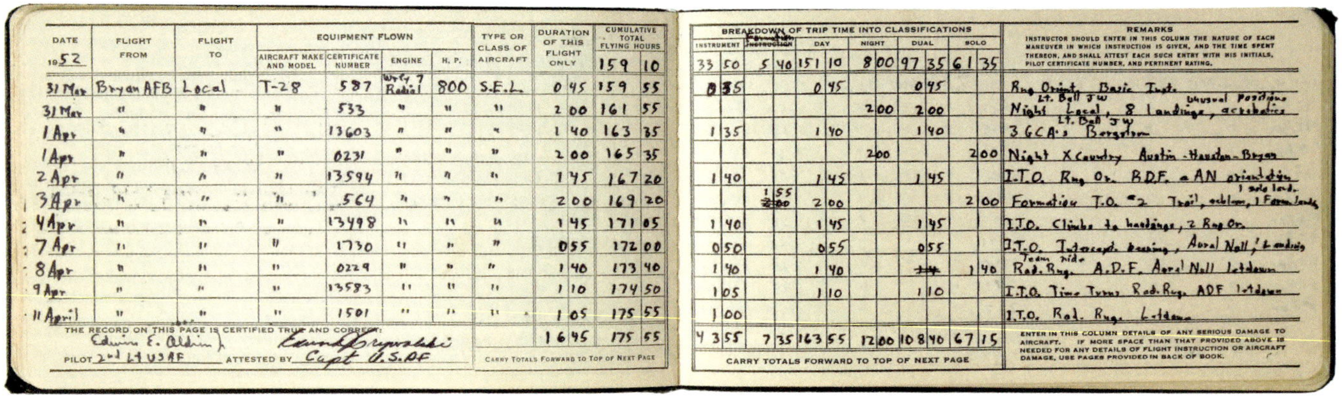

A spread from Buzz Aldrin's flight record and logbook during his time as a student pilot at Bryan Air Force Base. Courtesy of Heritage Auctions.

Ed White died, too, in a launch-pad fire during a preflight test of the *Apollo 1* capsule. He perished with Roger Chaffee and the mission's commander, Gus Grissom.

Grissom also spent time at Bryan Air Force Base. In fact, his youngest son, Mark, was born at the Bryan Air Force Base hospital in 1953.

In concluding a conversation with Buzz Aldrin, particularly on the RELLIS Campus site, it seemed fitting to ask him what advice he would give to students, themselves looking to reach out and touch the stars.

"Don't just settle for the steady. Look what the possibilities are," Aldrin said.

Extending his arms wide to either side of his body, he continued, "As you go through (life), you're going to reject a lot of things and you're going to accept some.

"Look at alternatives in life and be optimistic. Some good things will happen, and if they don't, don't get too discouraged. Look to the next opportunity.

"Things will get better, if you're in the right business, if you picked the right thing that's growing.

"If you didn't, get out and get into something else."

Buzz Aldrin (*right*) with *RELLIS Recollections* author Tim Gregg before their interview at the RELLIS Center for Infrastructure Renewal conference center. Photo by author.

Don Ho

Future astronauts weren't the only Air Force officers to make a name for themselves at the site that would one day become the RELLIS Campus.

Lieutenant General James Abrahamson served as an instructor at Bryan Air Force Base in the mid-1950s. He flew nearly 50 combat missions during the Vietnam War and later, as a general, was director of President Ronald Reagan's Strategic Defense Initiative. After retiring from the military, Abrahamson later served as an executive vice president for the Hughes Aircraft Company and was chairman of the board for the Oracle Corporation.

Donald Tai Loy Ho, *better known as Don Ho, was an American musician, singer, and entertainer. He is best known for the song "Tiny Bubbles." Born in Honolulu, Hawai'i, Ho grew up on the island of O'ahu. He attended college on a football scholarship in Springfield, Massachusetts, but returned home to earn a bachelor's degree in sociology from the University of Hawai'i. In 1954, Ho entered the United States Air Force. Following his tour of duty at Bryan Air Force Base, Ho was transferred to Travis Air Force Base near Concord, California, and it was there he bought an electric keyboard from a music store, which is how, he said, his career got started. Ho died in his home state of Hawai'i in 2007 at the age of 76.*

Courtesy of US Air Force.

And technically, Abrahamson *was* an astronaut. Following his military service in Southeast Asia, Abrahamson attended the Aerospace Research Pilot School at Edwards Air Force Base in California. After graduation there, he was named one of the 17 "astronauts" in the Air Force's Manned Orbiting Laboratory program. Six of those men—but not Abrahamson—were reassigned to NASA and flew into space after the Manned Orbiting Laboratory program was terminated in 1969.

While earthbound, musician Don Ho entertained millions of people around the world. Bryan businessman Louis Newman remembers seeing Ho perform in concert in Hawaii. Newman says he was impressed that Ho included mention of his military service in the United States Air Force, and then surprised that Ho spoke during his show of his time as a student pilot at Bryan Air Force Base . . . where he nearly died crash-landing a plane.

The website Military.com features an interview with Ho about his years as an Air Force pilot.

A Brush With Death in Texas

Q: What influenced your decision to join the Air Force?

Ho: I was enrolled in the ROTC at the University of Hawaii, and after graduating from there, I went to boot camp at Lackland Air Force Base (near San Antonio). Then, we went to Mayfair (near Sacramento, California). And then, we went back to Lackland. I got my primary training in Columbus, Mississippi.

Q: Can you describe the training?

Ho: The training began at the University of Hawaii, where we went through the basic, mental material, which was aerodynamics and so on. And then we trained in navigation. In Columbus, basically I went down to the line, and they put me in a plane with an instructor, and we took off, and the instructor told me to fly the plane. The training was precise, the instructors were very good, and they were very strict. They were all veterans from the war. We were lucky to get experienced personnel training us. The instructors were taking up green kids like us and they had to be firm. We were trained in PA-18s and T-6s for about six months, and then we went to Bryan, Texas, where we got training in T-28s and T-33s. After I graduated from there, I had basic training. The Korean War ended, and they didn't need fighter pilots, so I ended up coming home to Hickam (in Hawai'i) and flying the line between Travis Air Force Base (Concord, California) and Tokyo. We were the 27th Squadron out of Hickam. Then the squadron moved to Travis. I was stationed there for a couple of years.

Q: What were the PA-18 Trainers and the other planes like?

Ho: The PA-18s were fantastic airplanes. The PA-18s were Piper Cubs. The T-28s were fantastic planes too. The T-6s were reliable planes; they were good planes to land in, because if you could fly that plane, you could fly anything. The T-33s were incredible. As students, getting into a jet, it was everything we were looking forward to. I would recommend to every kid go and try to be a pilot. You get close to God real fast.

Q: What was it like when you crash-landed a T-33 in Texas?

Ho: I thought about God real quick, when I had to look for a place to crash-land. My whole life flashed before me in a split second, and then I pretty much relied on everything I knew, to survive that situation. I flew over a cornfield and trees into a barn with chickens, ducks, and cows. The plane was up flying again in a couple of weeks. It was a lucky landing. I had to crash-land because I had a flameout. I had a choice of bailing out or landing. I felt that I was better equipped to land the plane, then to jump out of it. I'm grateful that I was taught well. Proper procedures on how to crash-land an airplane. Of course, I was fortunate that I could crash on land and not in water.

Q: Did you do any combat flying? Did you ever fly in a storm?

Ho: No, I ended up flying the C-97s, which were the old Pan Am Strato-cruisers. They were also using those planes as tankers for refueling. I did have a scare in Columbus with a tornado. I was able to land on the ground in time.

Q: What advice can you offer to someone who may be interested in flying?

Ho: I'd say go for it. If you plan to go into the military, see if you can qualify to be a pilot. I didn't think I could ever do it. It will probably be one of the ultimate experiences in your life. My first time up in a plane, there was a feeling of confusion. I expected that I would get some instructions before I put my hands on the controls. The instructors just gave us the controls, and let us fly the planes.

Q: Have you applied your experiences in the Air Force to life in general?

A: My success in show business is completely predicated on my training in commanding the airplane. The work I do in entertainment, the people in my show, the way I run the show, is like I ran my flight crew in the Air Force. So we are well disciplined in my shows. I owe a lot to the training I had in the Air Force.

(From an interview with George Furukawa)

Mark Grissom on the RELLIS Campus flight line. Photo by author.

CHAPTER 11
Father's Footsteps

There was a time in America when a boy's interest turned to cars rather than computer games, smart-phone texts, or Instagram.

Fast cars, to be sure.

The summer of 1970 brought 16-year-old Mark Grissom back home. Back home to Bryan Air Force Base.

For many years, autocross events sponsored by the Texas A&M Sports Car Club were regularly held at the site of the present-day RELLIS Campus. Few other places featured as much unencumbered asphalt for amateur-driving enthusiasts, thanks to the multiple runways and flight line of the former military installation where pilots trained during two American wars.

A half century ago, Bryan-College Station had a lot to offer racing fans like Mark, a high school junior living in the suburbs of Houston's Clear Lake City area.

The Texas World Speedway opened its track here in 1969. Racing greats Al Unser, A.J. Foyt, and Richard Petty drove to wins there.

The Texas A&M Research Annex autocross rally, held at the former Bryan Air Force Base, gave Mark Grissom a chance to drive where his father had flown jets as a young instructor pilot in the final year of the Korean War.

Mark inherited his love of cars from his dad. As a kid, Mark was the envy of his young friends, thanks to his dad's Chevrolet Corvette. But it wasn't just any Corvette.

It was a right-off-the-production-line, second-generation 1963 Corvette Stingray, a perquisite for the job Gus Grissom held at the time.

Astronaut.

Mark Grissom was back in town on the 75th anniversary of the dedication of Bryan Army Air Field: June 6, 2018. He visited at the invitation of the Texas A&M University System's chancellor's office.

The A&M System, in an effort to preserve the history of the RELLIS Campus, seeks to honor the legacy of those who spent time at the site and achieved major accomplishments in their lifetimes. Gus Grissom is one of those people.

Tragically, his life was cut short.

Grissom died in a launch-pad accident preparing for the first Apollo spaceflight in the early weeks of 1967. In a twist of bitter irony, Grissom was one of three future astronauts previously stationed at Bryan Air Force Base to die in the line of space duty. Ted Freeman and Charlie Bassett perished in separate airplane crashes while training for space flight.

William Pogue and Buzz Aldrin also spent time in Bryan as cadet pilots. Pogue flew on NASA's Skylab 4 mission. Aldrin, the Apollo 11 Lunar Module pilot, walked on the moon.

The original Mercury Seven astronauts, a group which included Gus Grissom, quickly became national celebrities in the early 1960s. As interest in the "Space Race" grew, six-figure magazine deals and free cars from admiring auto dealers came along with that fame.

Grissom and fellow astronaut Gordon Cooper, car enthusiasts from childhood, bought into an Indianapolis 500 racing team while active in the astronaut program.

That sort of "largess" no longer exists for NASA's "star voyagers."

"People must remember the Mercury astronauts got just their military pay for pretty hazardous duty," Mark Grissom said of America's space pioneers, all of whom, including his father, came to the space program as military test pilots.

"Each one got a car as one of the 'benefits' of their new jobs," Mark remembered. "Except John Glenn, who turned down the offer."

According to Tom Wolfe's classic book, *The Right Stuff*, Glenn was known to his spacefaring compatriots as the "clean marine."

"(Wally) Schirra had a Ferrari, Scott Carpenter drove a Cobra, and 'Gordo' Cooper had a Ford Galaxy 500 with a 429-cubic-inch engine," Mark Grissom recounted.

Gus got the '63 Stingray from Indy 500 winner and Florida auto dealer Jim Rathmann, who later became the principal partner in the Grissom/Cooper racing team.

While Mark drove a 2007 Chevy pickup to his RELLIS homecoming, the other car in the garage of his Oklahoma City–area home is more in line with family tradition: a 2018 Sebring Orange Corvette.

Mark, indeed, has followed in his father's footsteps.

Mark Grissom was born at the Bryan Air Force Base hospital on December 30, 1953. He was the second son to First Lieutenant Virgil and wife Betty Grissom. During their just-over-a-year stay in the area, the Grissom family lived on Nagle Street near the Texas A&M campus.

Newly hired A&M football coach Bear Bryant lived around the corner on Greenway.

"Mom always talks about Coach Bryant being a neighbor," Mark said of his mother, who still calls Houston home.

"The other thing she remembers about living in Bryan was how low and ominous storm clouds seemed to her. She says she always felt like she could reach up and touch them."

The Air Force took the Grissom family from post to post after leaving Bryan. Once Gus became an astronaut, the family eventually moved to Houston.

"He was gone a lot as I was growing up," Mark said of his father. "In the Air Force, he frequently spent his weekends flying cross-country to earn additional flight pay. I think he got into that habit while stationed at Bryan Air Force Base."

Mark Grissom was 13 when his father died alongside fellow astronauts Ed White and Roger Chaffee. The tragedy left Mark, his mother, and his older brother, Scott, shocked, saddened, and somewhat secluded from the rest of the astronaut community. Denial of the extreme hazards awaiting those at the epicenter of the "Space Race" was a key component of coping with the unimaginable stresses, a part of the "right stuff."

Reminders of those hazards realized were not welcome. The Grissoms were somewhat ostracized.

Thus, the blue Camaro convertible in which Mark competed in autocross rallies as a teenager helped bring some sense of normalcy back into his young life.

Mark shared memories of his father on his visit to the RELLIS Campus.

"Whenever he was in town during his career as an astronaut," Mark said, "Dad would load up the car with neighborhood kids and we'd go to the drag strip, or an Astros game, or we'd all go duck hunting somewhere."

Above: Astronaut Gus Grissom with his youngest son Mark in front of their home near NASA's Manned Spacecraft Center near Houston. Courtesy of Mark Grissom.

Right: Mark Grissom spent the first months of his life with his parents and brother in this Bryan home on Nagle Street. Photo by author.

Mark is now 64, nearly a quarter-century older than his father was at the time the *Apollo 1* mishap occurred. Short but powerfully built, Mark bears a striking resemblance to his dad, although his hair is longer and flecked with gray.

Gus Grissom was known for his signature military-style flattop.

Also, unlike his dad, Mark wears glasses. He has for a long time.

And, to hear Mark tell it, those glasses prevented him from attending college at Texas A&M.

"I was offered an ROTC scholarship to come to school here," Mark said. "That was near the end of the Vietnam War. But I had bad eyes. Maybe not the worst, but not good enough to become a fighter pilot. So, I turned down the opportunity to join the Corps of Cadets."

While not following his father's footsteps into the Armed Forces, Mark eventually enrolled in his dad's alma mater, Purdue University. There, he pursued a professional pilot technology degree, determined to fly.

After college, Mark landed a series of aviation jobs, but none lasted. Eventually, he became an air-traffic controller at Oklahoma City's Will Rogers World Airport. He continues in that line of work today.

Mark's only child, son Cody, 24, also pursued an aviation career, serving as a first officer for American Eagle. He, too, is a Purdue graduate.

Before his 2018 return to the site of the old Bryan Air Force Base, Mark Grissom believed his last trip to the area had occurred more than 30 years ago.

The RELLIS campus, he said upon personal inspection, felt like familiar ground.

"I look around, I see the flight-control tower and the hangars and the old mess hall, and it's easy to imagine my dad being here."

Mark smiled as he looked out over the flight line from where his father once soared into the Texas sky and where, as a teenager himself, Mark weaved his '69 Camaro through a slalom course of road cones.

One had the sense Mark Grissom was, indeed, back home.

John A. Adams Jr.

John A. Adams Jr. is one of Texas A&M's most well-regarded and best-liked authors and historians. He has bachelor's, master's, and doctoral degrees from Texas A&M University.

Adams' introduction to Aggieland came thanks to the United States Air Force.

Squadron Commander's Son

"My father (was) assigned to Bryan Air Force Base in the early '50s, and so we moved to the base. He was a squadron commander. There were two duplexes there for residences and they were there until recently, used for training, SWAT training, for the police academy (TEEX Law Enforcement).

"I remember (my time there) vividly. I was five, six, seven years old. The base was wide open and those were the days before seat belts and child seats. I'd stand in the front seat of the car when we'd go out to the flight line and look at the airplanes, which is maybe why I have such a love for airplanes today.

"My dad loved to plant trees and so everywhere we went we planted trees. There really weren't many trees at all (at Bryan Air Force Base) since the land had been a cotton field before they moved the base there during World War II. So (my dad) planted trees around the house and they were there until they recently tore down our old home in the redevelopment of the RELLIS Campus.

"At the end of the road where we lived at Bryan Air Force Base there was a lake. Actually it was an artesian well and it was boiling hot water. I remember as a kid steam rising from the lake, especially when it got cool. The hot water would steam up and it would get fogged up there.

"Another thing that happened: a neighbor kid and I were riding a tricycle one day, and we saw what we thought was a rope in the middle of the street. We rushed back home, leaving the tricycle, to ask permission to take the rope. Well, when we got back, it turned out to be a rattlesnake and it was wrapped around the front and back of the tricycle! They had to call the air police over to get the snake. That story has been passed down through my family for generations now!

"Our family later lived in North Africa, Turkey, Panama, and Nicaragua, but when we could, we'd always come back here. We had friends here so we'd always come back through here. I was born in San Antonio. My brother was born while we were at Bryan Air Force Base in 1953. Actually, he was born in town at the Bryan Hospital. And so we always came back through here and every time we would come back here we would ride out to what we always called 'the base.' The name has changed through the years, but when we were back in town we'd always go out to 'the base' and ride through and go by and see the house, the duplex where we lived."

John A. Adams Jr. '73 *received a bachelor's degree, master's degree, and PhD in history from Texas A&M. Adams was a captain in the United States Air Force and served as president and CEO of Enterprise Florida Inc., a public/private-sector statewide economic development organization. Adams has served as an advisor to the World Trade Organization and has provided Congressional testimony on US-Mexico border infrastructure issues. He is the author of several books about Texas A&M University and the Corps of Cadets:* We Are the Aggies, Softly Call the Muster, Keepers of the Spirit, *and coauthor of* Texas Aggies Go To War.

Photo by author.

Cover of 1955 Bryan Air Force Base yearbook. From author's collection.

CHAPTER 12

The 1955 Bryan Air Force Base Yearbook

Yearbooks, we all have one . . . or more.

At least most of us probably do.

Anyone—everyone?—who has attended high school or college in this country (and likely other countries) probably has a yearbook, or "class book" as they were originally known, a collection of individual, group, action, candid, and, as the years go by, increasingly hysterical and potentially embarrassing photographs commemorating time spent in a communal educational environment.

Similar publications became popular in the military, too, dating as far back as World War II. In the Navy, "cruise books" chronicled ocean-fairing deployments and charted the missions' ports of call.

What might seem a nonessential task, particularly in times of war, yearbooks actually strengthened morale, reinforced purpose, and instilled pride in one's service to country by providing a permanent and lifelong reminder of patriotic duty.

I first became aware of the yearbooks produced at Bryan Air Force Base on a fact-finding trip to the Carnegie Library in downtown Bryan, Texas.

The helpful staff there was always eager to lend a hand or point me in the right direction. When I discovered the shelf with approximately two dozen Bryan Air Force Base yearbooks, I felt like I'd hit the mother lode.

I perused a few select volumes in an attempt to confirm the timeframe in which astronauts Buzz Aldrin and Gus Grissom were stationed at their Bryan post. Neither could be found in any of the yearbooks contained within the Carnegie collection.

Soon, I filed my Carnegie discovery in the "to-be-continued" category and moved on to exploring other facets of RELLIS Campus history in other places and with other people.

Then came one a memorable phone call.

Thanks to local media coverage of my quest for RELLIS Campus history, numerous people reached out to me to share their personal connection to RELLIS's past. Many of the stories derived from those contacts are now contained on the RELLIS Recollections website, with more to come.

But one voicemail in particular took me back in time . . . to the days of the popular cable television series, *The Sopranos*.

And, in fact, it was "Tony" who left the message.

The accent was unmistakably from the Jersey shore, but the Tony contacting me wasn't a product of the Soprano family tree. Instead, he was a descendant of the RELLIS line.

Tony Cordasco, retired and living today in Bryan, had seen the stories about my project and wanted to know if I'd be interested in taking a look at his 1955 Bryan Air Force Base yearbook.

In making my return call, I eagerly accepted Tony's invitation because I was intent on meeting the man.

I knew that airmen stationed at the base came from every corner of the country, and, assuming that Tony had been stationed there, he would be living proof of that geographic diversity.

Tony and Margaret Cordasco, married for 62 years, returned to the Brazos Valley to retire. She's originally from Bryan and met Tony while he was stationed at Bryan Air Force Base.

The Cordascos live in an attractive one-story brick home east of the Earl Rudder Freeway, just north of University Drive. Upon meeting Tony for the first time, he felt all he had to contribute to the RELLIS Recollections project was his yearbook.

Tony's story turned out to be about more than just the yearbook. His account of how he wound up at Bryan Air Force Base is contained in the sidebar section, "In Their Words," which follows this chapter.

Eventually, Tony let me borrow his yearbook What I found within its pages was something very different from most of the rest of the yearbooks from the post's past.

Unlike every other Bryan Air Force Base yearbook I've seen, the 1955 publication "has it all."

Other base class books feature photos of the command staff, instructors, cadets, and a few candid shots of base activities. Some have photos of Hollywood stars like Grace Kelly and Doris Day, personally signed to the "boys" at Bryan Air Force Base.

Upon closer inspection and comparison of those pages, I discovered that Kelly's handwriting is identical to that of Day, at least in the Bryan Air Force Base yearbook. I suspect those notes came from a civilian secretary on site willing to fudge the truth to boost base morale.

While there are no "pin-up models" in the 1955 book, the volume does include, remarkably in my mind, individual photos of almost every person who served in uniform or worked as a civilian on the base.

Included among the hundreds of head shots contained in the book were new friends and acquaintances I'd made in my pursuit of RELLIS history: Tony Cordasco himself, a young hospital corpsman during his short stay at Bryan Air Force Base; Regina Stetz, a youthful maintenance department secretary whose family farm just south of the base was spared from government seizure to build the facility during World War II.

And, included among a dozen or so civilian men working within the Maintenance Squadron's engine section, Louis Massey, who met and married Mary Kalinec while serving as an enlisted man at Bryan Army Air Field and then became a civilian mechanic there in the 1950s.

You've run across each of their stories within the pages of *this* book too.

The first A&M College of Texas yearbook, published in 1895, was named the *Olio*. Then, in 1903, a name change took place and for the next 46 years, the A&M annual was called the *Long Horn*.

Not long after the *Long Horn* became *Aggieland* in 1949, Bryan Air Field was opened and, a year later, in 1952, the first base yearbooks were released, a new volume produced for each training class that followed over the ensuing seven years.

All volumes were "spartan" compared to the 1955 annual that Tony shared with me.

Other Bryan Air Force Base yearbooks were called by a variety of other names: *Pitch Out*, derived from the aviation maneuver and not the baseball tactic; *Lima*, appropriately named for the 1955-L class that featured a young cadet by the name of Don Ho; *On The Go*, for the 1957-O class; and *Jet Stream*, the name embossed on the final Bryan Air Force Base yearbook publication for the I class of 1958.

Virtually all Bryan Air Force Base class books were student projects, managed and produced by cadet pilots or young administrative officers. In the 1952-D edition of *Pitch Out*, the editorial staff offered a full-page tribute to First Lieutenant John Porter "whose untiring efforts and wholehearted cooperation made this book possible." Porter, an instructor at the base and a member of the Tuskegee Airmen during World War II, contributed numerous illustrations used throughout the book.

Second Lieutenant Miles Fisher, a cadet pilot in "Orphan Flight," edited the last Bryan Air Force Base yearbook in 1958.

In a "letter from the editor and his staff (a six-person contingent responsible for copywriting, layout and soliciting advertisements from local businesses)," Fisher offered a lasting observation on his time at the post.

> *We wouldn't trade our experience for anything but we wouldn't go through it again on a bet. We've sweated our check rides, academic exams, military discipline, and physicals. As we have moved on we have had little time to look back at the many good men that left our ranks along the road. We've griped, complained, been discouraged, disheartened, angry and disappointed. The program really tested our patience and will power, but we stuck it out.*
>
> *Now as we leave this chapter of life behind us we begin to realize how much work, planning and money were necessary to make our training possible. Thousands of people have put in thousands of hours to get us through. Our flying and academic instructors put in the most effort for our training. However, military training personnel have worked out a lot of kinks and bad habits to make us sharp and responsible officers in the United States Air Force. Many others in the food service, supply, maintenance, hospital, transportation, administration and support units have given us constant aid in our endeavors to succeed as pilots.*
>
> *We the Class 58-I wish to take this opportunity to say "Thanks a lot for everything" to every person who has contributed to our training.*

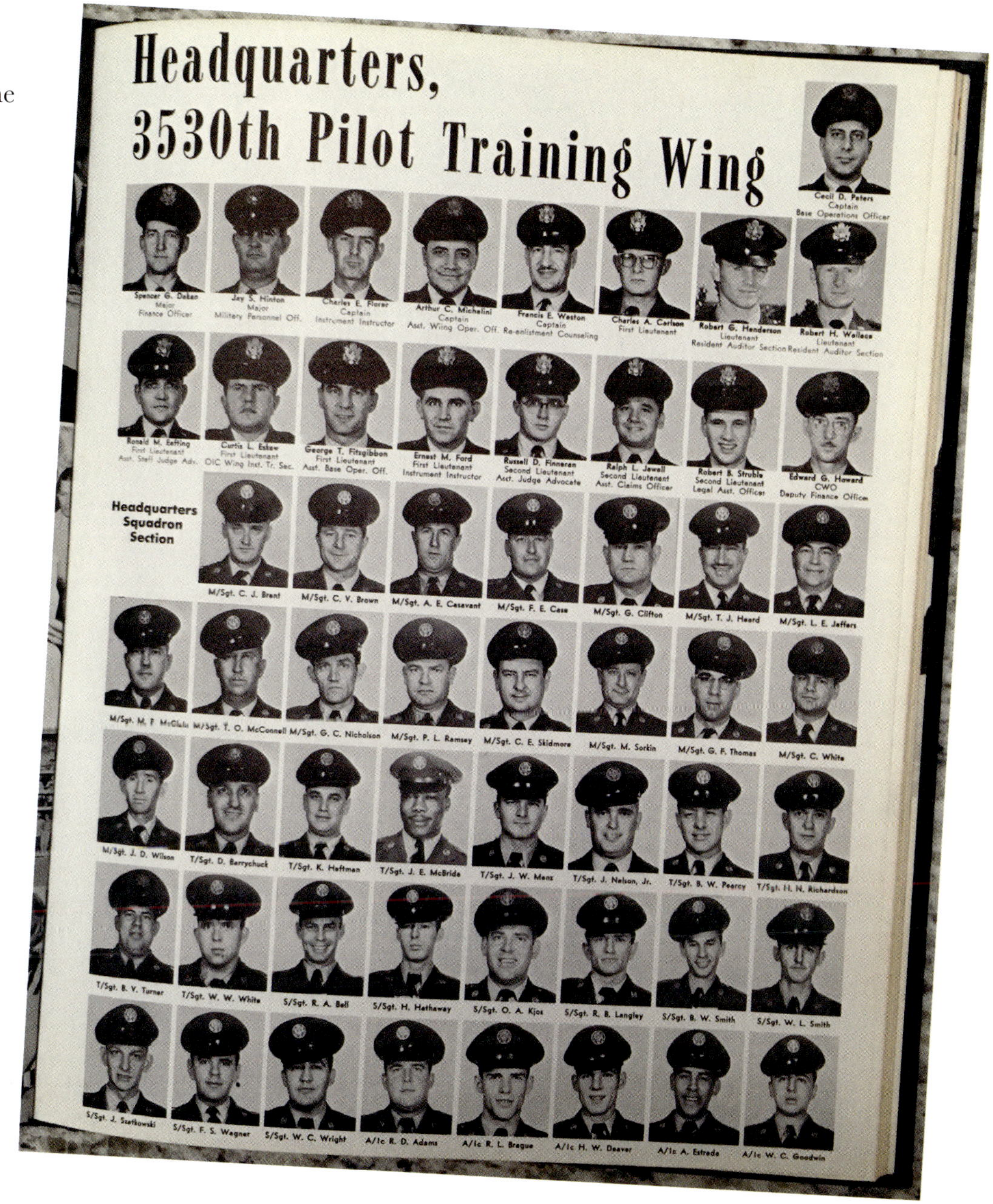

Right: A page from the 1955 yearbook, showing just a few of those who served the nation at Bryan Air Force Base. From author's collection.

Colonel James Gunn was commander of Bryan Air Force Base in 1955 and until the base's closing in 1958. He was also a World War II hero, facilitating the rescue of more than 1,100 POWs from a prison camp in Romania. From author's collection.

Competitive athletics, and other forms of recreational activities, were important morale boosters at every service post. From author's collection.

Tony Cordasco

For many young men reaching "legal age" in the 1940s and 1950s, the journey to manhood often was routed through a branch of the military. Service to country was not only a patriotic duty still embraced by most young Americans, but also, through the GI Bill, a practical means to a college education.

Tony Cordasco grew up in Camden County, New Jersey, just across the Delaware River from Philadelphia. Upon his graduation from Barrington High School, he saw the Armed Forces as an opportunity for a better life. His father, having served in the military himself, wasn't quite sure he wanted his son's life to chart the same course.

Jersey Boy

"I grew up in northern New Jersey and then in June 1954, I graduated high school. The Korean War was kind of on a lull then, so it was time for me to go into the Army, Air Force, Navy or something, and get on the GI bill. So, I went down to the Navy (recruiting office) and signed papers, but I was 17 years old then and I had to have my father sign for me.

"My father says, 'You know what, I'm not sure I want you to go into service. So, I'm going to give you this car, but I don't want you to drive it until I put the insurance on it.'

"Well, wouldn't you know it, later that same day I got in the car, drove a block from our house and hit a parked car while I was leaning over trying to fix the sun visor. I totaled that car.

"To make matters worse, there were two cops behind me. They put me in their squad car bleeding and took me to the hospital. I had a cut lip and bruised chest, so they didn't keep me there. I'm thinking, 'What am I going to do?' I know my dad isn't going to be very happy with me. I get out of the hospital and got on the bus and I went to my cousins'

Airman 3rd Class Anthony R. (Tony) Cordasco (*middle row, middle photo*) was a member of the Bryan Air Force Base hospital unit. From author's collection.

house. They're twins, about 12 years older than me, just out of the Navy. Jerry and Ralphie were their names and I told them I was pretty sure I was in a lot of trouble.

"So, about six in the evening, I hear footsteps coming up the porch there, and the next thing I know, '*badabing, badaboom*,' my father comes in and he was saying some 'nice' words. He tells me, 'You're gone! I'm singing the papers, but you're not going Navy, you're going Air Force!' The next day, August 19, 1954, I signed up.

"For ten weeks I was at Sampson Air Force Base in Geneva, New York. Then, I got orders—there were six of us who got the same orders—shipping me to Bryan Air Force Base in Texas. So, we got our bus and train tickets and off we go.

"We get to St. Louis, where we transferred, and everything was okay. Now we're going to Dallas. We had a layover there. We said, 'Let's go to the movies.' So, we went downtown to the movie house and we go to the ticket window and they tell us, 'No, you can't come in here.'

"I was with three young black airmen. I said, 'You can't do that!' meaning discriminate against my friends. Nothing like that ever happened back home in New Jersey or in New York. The next thing I knew, people were making a circle around us, out there in front of that movie house. The three guys said to me, 'Tony, we'll see you.' And they left. And, I'm carrying everyone's meal tickets.

"We eventually all got back onto the train and we made it to Bryan. Actually, we were at the college station (in College Station, adjacent to the A&M College campus). We were told to call the base when we got there, so we started putting money into the telephone. Up north, you put the money in first and then talked. In Texas, you talked, then put your money in. We were down to our last nickel before we got hold of someone at the base and they came and picked us up."

After leaving the military, **Tony Cordasco** *and his wife, Margaret, eventually settled in the Houston area. Tony worked for the US Postal Service for more than 30 years there, while Margaret owned and operated her own beauty salon. After retirement, the Cordascos moved back to Bryan to be close to their two children, five grandchildren, and one great-grandchild. An avid golfer, Tony has recorded six holes-in-one in his playing time at the former Travis B. Bryan Municipal Golf Course. His last ace came at the age of 80.*

Photo by author.

Aerial photo of Bryan Air Force Base inscribed with the handwriting of Travis B. Bryan in which the local banker denotes the impending closing of the field. Courtesy of Travis B. Bryan Family.

CHAPTER 13
Annexation

The closure of Bryan Army Air Field at the conclusion of World War II was a major economic blow to the local area.

Gone were the six-figure monthly payroll and contract services that provided significant financial benefit to local businesses.

Community leaders pushed hard to get the base operational again. The Korean War eventually made that possible.

The installation was reopened—under the name Bryan Air Force Base—on July 1, 1951, thanks in large part to the influence of local banker Travis B. Bryan.

But, Bryan, unknown to many, had an even more grandiose plan for the site.

In early 1950, the US Air Force announced its desire to establish an institution of higher learning and officer training similar to those for the Army at West Point, New York, and Navy at Annapolis, Maryland.

Three months later, Bryan had assembled a nearly 100-page brief on why the Bryan-College Station area of Central Texas would be an ideal place to locate the Air Force "Air Academy."

The case he made was compelling. In his 1948 Mother's Day letter to President Harry Truman, he had outlined a similar idea for members of the A&M Corps of Cadets.

By early 1954, a commission was finally created to begin the search for the academy's location. More than 580 sites were considered.

Texas A&M President Earl Rudder and U.S. President Lyndon Johnson. Courtesy of Cushing Memorial Library & Archives, Texas A&M University.

On June 24, 1954, Colorado Springs, Colorado, was selected as the academy's new home.

Travis Bryan was informed the Bryan-College Station area had finished "in the top five."

Four years later, on July 1, 1958, Bryan Air Force Base was permanently closed and the General Services Administration put the entire 2,000-acre venue up for sale. The initial asking price: $18 million. There were no buyers.

Then Lyndon Johnson stepped into the picture.

According to a story in the July 16, 1961, edition of *The Bryan Daily Eagle* newspaper, the vice president, a Texas native and long-time political powerhouse, announced he would ask the National Aeronautics and Space Administration (NASA) to give "serious consideration" to the Bryan Air Force Base site for the expansion of the nation's rapidly growing space program.

Shortly after Alan Shepherd became the first American in space on May 5, 1961, Bryan-College Station Chamber president Russell Hillier sent a letter to NASA officials reminding them the Bryan Air Force Base site sat vacant. One of its key assets, Hillier wrote, was proximity to the faculty, laboratories, and ongoing research activities at Texas A&M College.

In Johnson's public response to Hillier's letter, he vowed NASA would "definitely include the Bryan Air Force Base with those facilities to be evaluated for possible utilization in the space program."

Meanwhile, a separate search was underway to determine a location for NASA's Manned Spacecraft Center. Congressional appropriations earmarked more than $60 million for the facility. By late summer of 1961, 23 locations, not including Bryan Air Force Base, had been reviewed by a site-selection panel. Tampa's MacDill Air Force Base was the group's top choice.

As vice president, Johnson was head of the National Space Council, which oversaw all NASA activity. He was determined NASA's new spaceflight headquarters would be located on Texas soil.

Ultimately, it was.

The Manned Spaceflight Center—now called the Johnson Space Center—was established 25 miles southeast of downtown Houston near the mostly barren area today called Clear Lake, a place hundreds of astronauts eventually would call home.

While Johnson's announced support for Bryan Air Force Base generated much excitement in the Bryan-College Station area, a full-scale NASA connection never materialized.

Russell Hillier had a longer view of the executive "endorsement."

"The vice president's letter," Hillier said, "points out to me that everyone on the local level . . . should be devoted to acquiring the facilities at Bryan Air Force Base for Texas A&M College. (The base) would make an excellent research park for Texas A&M where research-oriented industry could prosper and grow."

Hillier added that an infusion of research scientists at the venue could bolster the local economy by several million dollars each year.

Hillier, it turned out, was not alone in those sentiments.

On August 28, 1961, A&M's board of directors authorized school president Earl Rudder "to do any and all things necessary and proper to procure and accept Bryan Air Force Base for transfer by the Department of Health, Education and Welfare (to) the Agricultural and Mechanical College of Texas."

For months, Rudder had been working to turn around the fortunes of his school. Enrollment was stagnant and faculty morale was on the decline. An independent study suggested several reasons for the increasing malaise, chief among them: limited scope of available curricula and compulsory military training for the male-only student body.

The institution's official designation as a "college" rather than a "university" also negatively impacted public perception.

Lyndon Johnson urged Rudder to adapt to the times.

Bryan Air Force Base turned out to be Rudder's first step toward modernizing his school.

Texas Senate Bill 1 already had given A&M permission to seek use of the base's facilities, with one caveat. The bill prohibited use of general revenue funds to facilitate a purchase or lease agreement.

Fortunately, the asking price would be lowered. Dramatically.

In an effort to rid the federal government of excess property, the Department of Health, Education and Welfare offered A&M a potential 100-percent discount on purchase of the site. The deal stipulated that each year the school made productive use of the facility, the price for the property would be reduced by five percent.

Thus, no money would be required for A&M to gain control and eventually ownership of the installation.

Annexation officially took place at the main gate of Bryan Air Force Base on May 1, 1962.

Sam Wynn, regional representative of the federal government's Division of Surplus Property, presented the deed to Eugene Darby, president of A&M's board of directors. Darby then handed over the paperwork to Rudder.

Aggie lore suggests that, in return, Rudder gave Wynn a $10 bill.

A sign unveiled at the entrance that day read: "Research Development Annex of A&M College."

In justifying the remarkable arrangement, Wynn cited the importance of the educational research that would soon take place at the site.

"The benefits gained from this usage far exceed the amount of money that we could have obtained from an open sale," he said.

Also on hand for the annexation ceremony were Russell Hillier and an aging Travis B. Bryan.

"This presents us with a golden opportunity to see industry, agriculture, commerce, and education work hand in hand," Hillier said.

Hillier told reporters he believed it would take "a long time to bring about big changes at the site" but that he was confident the "new annex" would produce many rewards for the area.

Today, anyone driving past the former Research Annex west of Bryan can see Hillier's vision being fully realized in the development of the Texas A&M University System's RELLIS Campus.

A promising future finally realized.

Bob Rudder

While Earl Rudder helped strike the deal in which the old Bryan Air Force Base became a part of Texas A&M College, the youngest of his five children, Bob Rudder, actually worked at the post, later to be called the Riverside Campus, for 15 years until retiring in 2017.

Family Legacy

"The first time I came with my dad out to the 'Annex,' as it was called back then, was when I was 'a single-digit' in age. That was probably in the early '60s. We came in through the main entrance off (Highway) 21 and went by the old guard shack. Dad wanted to teach me some shooting. So we came out and went through all that—there was no gun range at the time—and then we drove around to see what was out here. Dad wanted to get a better idea of what was going on after the university acquired the property.

"Dad became good friends with President Johnson when we lived in Brady. Dad worked on one of Johnson's political campaigns and he and dad became friends through the years. I remember the first time we visited the president's ranch. We drove through Johnson City (Texas) and went over to the property and met the president, who gave us a tour of the ranch. We started at the ranch house where LBJ grew up and out on the covered front porch area was a phone hanging on the wall, an old hand-cranked phone.

"I forget who told me, whether it was Dad or LBJ, but they said that the phone went straight to the operator at the White House. I was kind of like, 'Oh, come on!' And so they boosted me up and I got the earpiece and cranked the handle and all of a sudden this voice came on the line and said, 'White House.' I don't think I said a word because I was in shock. It was a neat experience.

"We then rode around. LBJ had an old Lincoln convertible with suicide doors on the back. We rode around the pastures in that—the roads were paved—and looked at his cattle. It was a really neat experience being away from the political side of it and seeing LBJ in a different light.

"I came to work at the Riverside Campus—now the RELLIS Campus—in about 2001 and stayed here for about 16 years. My title was "facilities coordinator," sort of the jack-of-all-trades and master of none. My job was to help if something needed attention or if somebody needed assistance, I tried to make things happen so we could get things accomplished.

***Bob Rudder** is the youngest of former Texas A&M President Earl Rudder's five children. He was born in Brady, Texas, but soon the family moved to Austin, where Rudder assumed the position of Texas Land Office Commissioner. Bob was five when Rudder was appointed "president-in-waiting" at A&M. Bob Rudder spent nearly 40 years working for the university his father helped make great. He makes his home in the Bryan-College Station area.*

Photo by author.

“The base chapel, which is still out there, was a meeting area and I handled reservations when people wanted to use it. I also coordinated use of the runways and taxiways. We had a reservation process for that. The USDA did crop-duster research and they were the only ones allowed to use the runways for aircraft. The Texas Transportation Institute built barricades and tested those (with vehicle crash tests on the runway complex). Everybody was kind of uncertain what was going to happen when I came on board, but as time went by, I’d like to believe they were convinced that I was here to help and not to hinder.

“I spent a lot of time driving the grounds just to see what was going on and frequently I’d come across people driving around who obviously didn’t know where they were going. I’d typically stop and talk to them. If they had business out here, I could point them in the right direction. If they didn’t, I would politely ask them to leave. But sometimes I would run into an individual that was stationed out here during one of the wars. That was one of the most enjoyable and informative parts of my job. If I wasn’t too busy and they were having a hard time figuring out where things were, I’d have them get in my vehicle and drive around . . . and tell me what they remembered.

“I worked 20 years on the main campus in the petroleum engineering department as a research associate. When I moved out to Riverside, it was like a small town. I knew most everybody and a lot of them became friends. They’d poke fun at me, calling me ‘mayor.’ The atmosphere out there was laid back, easy going, and you met some great people.

“Even though it was called ‘Riverside,’ the (Brazos) river wasn’t easy to find. There’s a pasture you’d go through on the south side of the property and I finally had to have one of the people working in a veterinary group there show me the way. I (went there) a couple times. It was really pretty with a steep drop-off down to the river.

“The other pretty view was from the top of the old flight control tower. The first time I went up there was with somebody that knew about the architecture of the buildings. It was interesting to hear how everything was built during World War II. Everything was designed to be disassembled and moved. In the hangars you had these massive wood beams which were bolted together and then could be unbolted to move, but never have. The second time I went up (the tower), I took as many pictures as I could. The top is two stories, one where people worked to watch for aircraft and then below that were the electronics that controlled the radios and all the lights for the runways.

“Eventually, they gutted the structure, put a fence around it with a lock, and so now it’s basically a shell of what it used to be, but at least it’s still there.”

Dick Zimmer at the site of a recent TTI crash on the RELLIS Campus proving grounds. Courtesy of Dick Zimmer. Photo by author.

CHAPTER 14
Crash Tests

On the Sunday afternoon of July 20, 1969, Dick Zimmer sat behind the steering wheel of his VW Bug, driving east along the Texas stretch of Interstate Highway 10.

Zimmer and his wife, Reta, had left their home in Las Cruces, New Mexico, that morning for College Station, Texas, where Dick would be interviewing for a position with the Texas Transportation Institute.

As he drove, Zimmer kept fussing with his car's radio dial. He was eager to locate coverage of that afternoon's Apollo 11 moon landing. He had a very personal interest in the historic mission.

But as he tuned up and down the AM dial, mostly what he found while traversing the sparsely populated high-desert country of West Texas was static.

Finally, Zimmer landed on the clear-channel frequency of WOAI radio in San Antonio. Although the signal faded in and out, the Zimmers sat silently, spellbound by the events unfolding nearly 250,000 miles away.

Unlike most Americans, Dick and Reta Zimmer had more than a passing fascination with the culmination of America's quest to land men on the moon. Each day, the space program had directly touched their lives.

For more than a year, Dick had worked for the Zia Company, one of the thousands of NASA contractors enlisted to support America's quest to win the "Space Race." Dick worked in the group testing the ascent engine of the lunar lander at the White Sands Missile Range in New Mexico.

His small part in the colossal undertaking of putting the first humans on the moon helped ensure that astronauts Neil Armstrong and Edwin "Buzz" Aldrin could safely make the return trip home.

And if the mission was accomplished, successfully, Zimmer knew the Zia contract would not be renewed.

Thus the long drive to find a new job.

The Apollo 11 moon landing was indeed a success and, fortunately, TTI hired Zimmer later that same year.

Now called the Texas A&M Transportation Institute, TTI's testing site remains located, as it was when Zimmer first began working for the agency, on the grounds of the former Bryan Air Force Base, now called the RELLIS Campus.

Zimmer has spent nearly 50 years with TTI conducting full-scale vehicle crash tests on roadside safety devices. But not until recently did Zimmer realize the additional connection he shares with one of the moonwalkers he helped bring safely home.

Buzz Aldrin spent, roughly, 90 days at Bryan Air Force Base in the first months of 1952, preparing to become a fighter pilot, a significant step on his personal journey to the moon and back home to earth, thanks in part to Dick Zimmer.

Zimmer's job with the Zia Company saw him assisting in the maintenance and operation of the test stand on which the Lunar Excursion Module's ascent-stage engine was fired.

"A 'full-scale' test meant they would put a full-size lunar lander into a large vacuum chamber," explained Zimmer. "The vacuum was created by the firing of three X-15 engines. In those tests, the LEM engine would ignite and burn for several minutes.

"It wasn't our job to assess the outcome of the tests," Zimmer added, "but to see that they were conducted correctly."

Each of the six lunar landers that ferried astronauts to the surface of the moon successfully returned their crews to orbiting Command Modules for the trip back to earth.

"We safety got our astronauts home," Zimmer said. "I'm proud of that."

Dick Zimmer has remained in the "safety" business ever since.

"My Air Force supervisor, who had helped me get the job in New Mexico, went to work for TTI," Zimmer shared.

"He wanted me to be a part of his team again, developing instrumentation systems for vehicle crash-testing."

Zimmer began working for TTI in November 1969. He has yet to fully retire.

"I started out as an instrumentation specialist," Zimmer said from the floor of TTI's historic World War II-era hangar building which serves now as a giant garage for the agency's work in Roadside Safety and Physical Security.

"What we did," Zimmer recalled of his initial days with TTI, "was mostly crash testing," a reasonably new pursuit in the quest for greater highway safety.

"In order to collect data from those tests, we had to develop our own equipment. That was before integrated circuits, before high-speed computers. We used resistors and capacitors and transistors. Real 'low-tech' stuff."

Since 1965, more than 3,000 full-scale crash tests have been conducted at TTI's Proving Grounds Research Facility on the RELLIS

Dick Zimmer, right, assesses crash-test results with a fellow engineer at the Texas Transportation Institute's facility on the site of the Texas A&M Research Annex. Courtesy of Dick Zimmer.

Campus. Most of those tests have taken place on the old runways of the former military base. Those tests have been critical in the development and refinement of highway-safety devices—such as guardrails, breakaway signs, and barrier systems—designed to make America's roadways safer for motorists.

Today, on-board high-speed digital recorders preserve the abundant and critical information to be gathered in a vehicular-crash scenario. A laptop computer connected to the "blue box" downloads the data.

Technology has come a long way under Dick Zimmer's watch.

"What we first had was a piece of cable coming out of the back of the vehicle, strung out about a thousand feet to a small trailer that had a tape recorder running on the other end. The test vehicle would get up to speed and crash into whatever we were testing and then the cable would follow, swishing back and forth until it piled up under the test car or truck."

Although no quarter-million-mile cables were needed, it still boggles the mind to consider that the same basic technology Zimmer used in the early days of collecting crash-test data for TTI was also employed in sending humans to the moon.

And as historically significant as those journeys were—highlighting America's "Space Age" achievements—the studies that Zimmer and his TTI associates continue to perform well into the "Information Age" have had an impact on "all mankind" too.

"We're definitely in the 'survival' business," Zimmer said, "making vehicular travel as safe as possible."

As for what keeps Zimmer "hanging around" TTI after all these years, he credits an atmosphere of creative support.

"I've had great bosses that gave me the freedom to try out crazy ideas," Zimmer said. "They were okay if I made a few mistakes and, if required, they would go to the administration for additional funding."

Zimmer first learned of his local connection to Buzz Aldren only last year after members of the team working on the redevelopment of the RELLIS Campus began looking for matters of historical significance at the site.

There is no question of Aldrin's place in history, both locally and intergalactically, but Dick Zimmer and the Texas A&M Transportation Institute deserve recognition, too, given the countless lives saved on global highways from controlled crash tests performed at the RELLIS Campus site.

Dick Zimmer in his Texas A&M Transportation Institute office nearly 50 years after his arrival at what is now the RELLIS Campus. Photo by author.

The Annual Reports

While chairman of the A&M College Board of Directors in 1912, Colonel Edward Benjamin Cushing personally bankrolled the school during a financially precarious time, preventing a proposed A&M consolidation with the University of Texas.

As a son of the owner of the Houston *Telegraph* newspaper, Cushing had the financial means to rescue his *alma mater*.

For that, and bequeathal of his collection of engineering books, A&M's first library, built in 1930, was named in Cushing's honor.

Today the Cushing Memorial Library and Archives are the historic repository for all important archival material relating to Texas A&M. Without question, its most important resources pertaining to the history of the RELLIS Campus are the "annual reports" filed as part of the 20-year "lease-to-own" arrangement between the school and the federal government's Department of Health, Education and Welfare.

With the mothballed Bryan Air Force Base sitting vacant for three years and no prospective buyers of the property on the horizon, the General Services Administration chose to lease the base to A&M in 1962.

In an initial "Reappraisal and Operational Study" of the deal, conducted by the college, terms of the agreement were outlined.

> "Texas A&M accrues title each year to one-twentieth of the total value of the property. Based upon the appraisal value of $3.6 million at the time of acquisition, an equity valued at $180,000 (disregarding depreciation) is earned each year."

The appraised value was far below the government's previous asking price of about $18 million. But to earn that discounted equity on the site, productive use of the base and its infrastructure had to be made and chronicled each year.

By year 4, in the autumn of 1966, the Texas A&M Research Annex "Annual Report" had landed on language that would be repeated as the document's "introduction" for the next decade.

> "Splendid Benefits"
>
> The Fourth Annual Report is submitted to the Department of Health, Education and Welfare by the Texas A&M Research Annex, a part of Texas A&M University.
>
> The Texas A&M Research Annex provides facilities for various university departments to perform both teaching and research activities. Because of space limitation on the main campus, the Annex has afforded excellent opportunities for expansion of existing programs as well as the creation of new ones. Also, several research programs considered too dangerous to the welfare of the people on the main campus are now operating in facilities ideal for such programs.
>
> The facilities are extremely advantageous for the students and faculty members who use them. Many students are now earning a livelihood by working on sponsored research projects, many of which may not now be active projects had it not been for the availability of the Annex facilities. Members of the faculty are benefitted by their participation in various research projects, enabling them to receive wider training and experience in their fields.
>
> Evidence of the splendid benefits derived from the acquisition of the Annex by Texas A&M University is apparent in Section I of the report titled, "Educational and Research Activities." Section II, III, and IV all concern specific statistical information required by the Department of Health, Education and Welfare.

Featured in the reports were assessments of the Texas Engineering Experiment Station's Activation Analysis and Chemurgic Research Laboratories; the College of Engineering's Electric Power Institute and Engineering Test Laboratory; the Space Technology Division's Propeller Static-Thrust Facility and Hypervelocity-Acceleration Laboratory; and the Texas Engineering Extension Service's Institute of Electronic Science, Industrial Radiographers School, Telephone Technicians Training School, and Polygraph Examiner's School.

The Texas Transportation Institute, as well as the A&M College of Agriculture Woody Plant Nursery, Animal Science Department, Range Science Department, and Department of Wildlife Sciences, also conducted tests and research activity on the Research Campus site, as did the Department of Veterinary Medicine and Surgery.

The twentieth—and final—annual report from the "Texas A&M Bryan Research and Extension Center"—as the site was then called—indicated usage of the site had expanded to include

US Department of Agriculture
Petroleum Engineering
Geology
Oceanography
Nautical Archaeology
Biology
Physics
College of Education
Texas Agriculture Extension Service
Texas Agriculture Experiment Station

The final report introduction reads as follows:

> On April 30, 1982, Texas A&M University completed twenty (20) years of beneficial utilization of the former Bryan Air Force Base. This facility has been extensively utilized by Texas A&M University and various parts of the Texas A&M University System for teaching, research, and extension during the twenty-year period extending from May 1, 1962, to April 30, 1982.
>
> The following material provides the Twentieth Annual Report on the use of the former Bryan Air Force Base and covers the time period from September 1, 1981, to April 30, 1982. The activity during this eight-month period was essentially a continuation of activity reported in the Nineteenth Annual Report.

By the final report, benefits were no longer described as "splendid." But terms of the original agreement had been executed and title to the property was signed over to the university's board of regents, whose name had changed from "board of directors" in 1975.

The Texas A&M Research Annex hosted a wide range of activities during the two decades of the school's "lease-to-own" arrangement with the federal government. These included an electronics school, animal husbandry studies, utility-worker training, and vehicular crash tests. (*Left to right*): Courtesy of Cushing Memorial Library & Archives, Texas A&M University (first three photos) and the Texas A&M Transportation Institute.

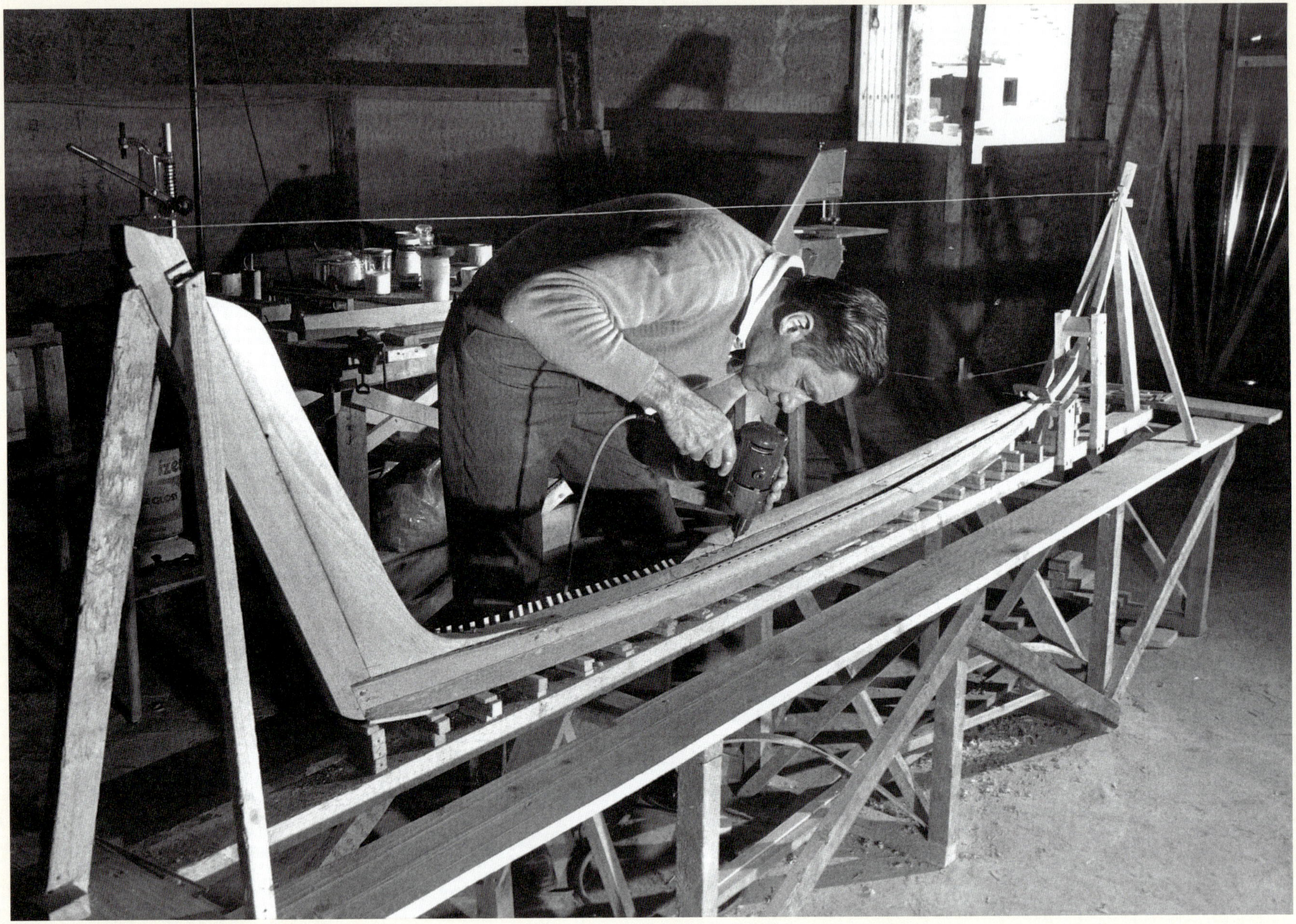

Dick Steffy at work on a ship model in the Nautical Archaeology Ship Lab located on the Research Annex campus. Courtesy of Loren Steffy.

CHAPTER 15

Ship Lab

The Texas A&M Ship Reconstruction Laboratory, unique among American universities, got its start in an old military barracks at what is now the RELLIS Campus.

Through the years, the "Ship Lab" has been a place where "ship-building through time" is studied and advanced using a wide range of methods, from hands-on modeling to computer simulations.

When A&M launched its Nautical Archaeology Program in 1976, a lack of space on the main campus pushed the ship lab into a forgettable building at the school's Research Annex on the outskirts of town.

J. Richard Steffy, the lab's founding director and "Dick" to his friends and students, was elated with the setup, despite its humble appearance.

The former Army barracks structure was a definite improvement over the two-car garage of his College Station home where he had held labs during his first year at the school.

According to the Texas A&M College of Anthropology website, nautical archaeology "is the study of the remains of boats and ships and the cultures that created and used them."

Right: Dr. Richard Steffy and associate, Dr. George Bass, at an event honoring Steffy's achievements with the Institute of Nautical Archaeology, which Bass founded in the 1960s and moved to Texas A&M in 1975. Courtesy of Institute of Nautical Archeology.

How Dick Steffy turned that interest as a long-standing personal hobby into a university teaching and research position, while earning for himself and Texas A&M an international reputation in the field—all while he had no more than a technical-school education—is one of the most remarkable stories in the annals of RELLIS history.

Texas A&M's Nautical Archaeology Program came to the university in 1976, part of a package deal along with the Institute of Nautical Archaeology. The institute's headquarters remain on campus, just down the hall from today's Nautical Archaeology home in the Ship Reconstruction Laboratory of the A&M Anthropology Building.

Both the program and the institute were the vision of Dr. George F. Bass, a pioneer in the field of underwater archaeology.

In 1960, while still a doctoral student at the University of Pennsylvania, Bass directed the first complete subaqueous excavation of an ancient shipwreck. That achievement, off the coast of Turkey, led to funding from a wide range of sources, including the National Geographic Society. The eastern Mediterranean Sea became the focal point of Bass's research, given the preponderance of centuries-old sunken vessels there.

Bass's 1963 *National Geographic* magazine article on the excavation of a Byzantine shipwreck near the Turkish island of Yassi Ada caught the attention of a model-boat enthusiast who had long been fascinated by ancient ships.

For nearly 20 years, Dick Steffy had worked at his father's electrical contracting business in the small southeastern Pennsylvania town of Denver. In his spare time, Steffy constructed ship models, winning prizes at hobby shows for the intricate details he crafted into his replicas of ancient boats.

After returning home from World War II, Steffy sought to further his education under the GI Bill, but his dreams of "big engineering projects" gave way to his responsibilities as a husband and father and the financial stability found working at his father's side.

Then, within the pages of *National Geographic*, Steffy found a kindred spirit in George Bass. He wrote Bass what amounted to a "fan letter."

"He asked me if he could make a model of the ship featured in the article," Bass recently said from his Bryan-College Station area home.

That request triggered what would become a lifelong partnership between the two men.

Bass discovered that Steffy was no "mantelpiece" model-maker. Despite a lack of formal education, Steffy took seriously his study of ancient vessels, and his long hours working on models offered an advancement in thinking from almost anything that had been done to that point in the academic world.

When Bass became a professor at Penn, he called upon Steffy to assist in his seminar on ancient seafaring. Ten years later, and thanks to Bass, Steffy was holed up in a seaside castle on the coast of Cyprus, successfully reconstructing the hull of a 2,300-year-old ship from its excavated remains.

Steffy had taken his modeling hobby to the extreme and was accomplishing something, scientifically, that had never been done before.

About that same time, in 1972, Bass launched the American Institute of Nautical Archaeology. With numerous projects in Cyprus, Bass initially based his institute there, but soon the nation erupted into civil war, destabilizing the region and throwing Bass's plans into disarray.

Stymied at every turn, Bass moved to Denver. By that time, Steffy had joined the institute full-time, and relocating to the Pennsylvania town enabled, as Bass said later, "at least one of us—Dick's wife—to hold down a steady job."

Despite his previous ties to Penn, Bass opted not to return to the Ivy League school. A colleague had a friend at Texas A&M and suggested Bass reach out to the football-mad Southwestern Conference university, which was looking to make a name for itself in places other than Kyle Field.

Bass's inquiries were eagerly received by A&M officials. Soon the school offered to host the institute, suggesting "America" be dropped from the name to give it a more international flavor. The university also hoped Bass could put together a graduate program in nautical archaeology.

There was one catch. Bass was adamant that Dick Steffy join him in Texas, but Steffy's lack of educational credentials—not even a bachelor's degree—meant he would not be able to teach at the school. Bass insisted an exception be made on behalf of his friend.

"I pointed out that Dick was unique," Bass said, "having been the first person in the world to reassemble for display in a museum the hull of an ancient ship. Dick was already lecturing around the country for the Archaeological Institute of America and was rated one of its best speakers."

Bass knew A&M was aggressively building its liberal arts college. The university eventually accepted Steffy as a member of its faculty, but with few privileges.

Loren Steffy is Dick's son. He's also one of Texas A&M's most accomplished journalism graduates. As a reporter for the *Houston Chronicle*, Loren Steffy broke major stories on both the downfall of Enron and the BP Oil disaster in the Gulf of Mexico.

He has written a book about his father, titled, *The Man Who Thought Like a Ship*, published by the Texas A&M University Press.

"His students in those first years, out at what's now the RELLIS Campus, told me his class was unlike anything they'd ever taken," Loren Steffy said.

"Keep in mind, my dad had never been in a real college classroom! So, he taught the way he would have wanted to be taught himself, very hands on and tactile.

"The lab was where, my dad believed, the ships started talking to him. It was in his lab, alongside his graduate students, where he tested theories on the reconstruction of excavated ship remains."

In 1985, Dick Steffy received the prestigious MacArthur Foundation Fellowship, otherwise known as a "genius grant." He eventually became a tenured professor at A&M, but, to his death in 2007, he never grew comfortable with his students calling him "Dr. Steffy."

The Nautical Archaeology Program moved onto the main campus in 1992. The ship lab that Steffy conceived and shaped now bears his name.

And the program that he and George Bass started together on the grounds of today's RELLIS Campus remains at the forefront of international scientific thought.

Steffy teaching graduate students. Courtesy of Loren Steffy,

Robert Brick

A surprisingly large number of individuals who grew up in the Bryan-College Station area have fond recollections of childhood trips to Bryan Air Force Base to go swimming. Of the two pools there, one was restricted to officers, but the other was open not only to all enlisted men but also their families and friends too, regardless of color.

In the 1950s at a time when Bryan, Texas, was still a segregated community, that pool was one of the few places where all people could mix and mingle.

After the base closed, the property was annexed by Texas A&M in 1962. While much of the base was put to use by the college, the enlisted-men's pool sat abandoned . . . until a young A&M professor by the name of Robert Brick was given the keys to the venue to conduct his research.

Shrimp Lab

"In 1975, I had just finished my graduate study at the University of Hawai'i and I joined the faculty of Wildlife and Fisheries Sciences at Texas A&M University. My specialty was in aquatic animal husbandry and the study of aquatic animal nutrition.

"I had two research facilities provided to me when I first joined the department. One was at what was then called the Research Annex. It was the old swimming pool for what had been the Bryan Air Base many years before. And it seemed appropriate to the authorities at the time that someone who was interested in growing fish and shrimp would have the outdoor swimming pool as his research facility.

"Actually, by that time it was a 'derelict' pool, simply a hole in the ground.

"That swimming pool had an old dressing room adjacent to it, a men's dressing room on one end and the women's on the other. It was a cinderblock building of not very great dimensions but it had a lot of height to it, so it was adequate for what we needed to do at that time, just getting started with a research program.

"My first impression of that dilapidated-looking dressing room was, 'Good grief what are we ever going to do with this?' But my students and I got together and scratched our heads and decided we needed a place in which we could keep our research animals over winter, keep

***Dr. Robert Brick** is a first-term city councilman for the City of College Station. In addition, Brick serves as a biological science research specialist for the Texas A&M Institute for Quantum Science and Engineering at the university's Salter Research Farm. Brick holds advanced degrees from the University of Hawai'i and a bachelor's from Texas Tech University. Dr. Brick has taught biology and zoology and previously served as a division chair at Blinn College. He is married to former Blinn College professor and College Station city councilwoman Blanche Brick.*

Courtesy of Robert Brick.

them alive and going during the cold season. So we began to work to convert the dressing rooms into an indoor research facility in which we had a recirculating water system: salt water on one side and fresh water on the other side. We needed those types of facilities to keep freshwater shrimp and saltwater shrimp alive.

"Well, it took us about two years to get the facility up and running and serviceable for what we needed. And so, after we got it up and running, we would grow our shrimp. The freshwater shrimp would be harvested at the end of summer and taken into our indoor facility before cold weather set in. They are a tropical species and they would die over winter if left outside. The saltwater shrimp that we brought up from the coast also did not do well in the cold season up here. But, for our purposes, for research purposes, we had to keep them at warm temperatures so we heated the water. We (couldn't) afford to heat water and dump it out when it was used and then bring in new water and reheat it. That was economically unfeasible. So we had to recirculate our water to keep it at the right temperature.

"I think (the work we did) was important at the time. There was an initiative, and I was a part of that, to introduce freshwater shrimp farming activity to Texas. We would bring in 'post larvae,' less than a half inch long shrimp larvae that had come out of the hatchery. You could purchase these at the time and stock them into a facility early in the season before it was warm enough to put them outdoors and could keep them indoors and let them grow up a little bit such that when you did take them outdoors they were larger and ready to go out into the ponds.

"This had been a practice I had done during my graduate research at the University of Hawai'i. The state there had promoted a freshwater shrimp farming program. And one of my tasks was to bring that to Texas and introduce that around. There are some remnants of that still in operation today. You can find freshwater shrimp programs here and there. (They're) not as prolific as I would have hoped at the time, but one outcome of the research that I did at the Research Annex was our 'recirculating dressing-room facility.'"

David Woodcock (*left*), founder of he Texas A&M Center for Heritage Conservation, and Jerry Gaston, former chairman of the Teas A&M Campus Facilities Planning Committee, stand in front of he new Texas A&M Transportation Institute building on the RELLIS Campus. Photo by author.

CHAPTER 16

Riverside Campus Master Plan

Highway 47 is no longer the road to the Riverside Campus.

After many years, the exit sign off Highway 60 near Easterwood Airport has been updated, proclaiming that 47 now heads toward the "TAMUS RELLIS Campus," reflecting the name change of the Texas A&M University System venue that occurred in 2016.

I remember the first time I saw that sign, in the summer of 2017, shortly after my wife and I moved to the College Station area.

It still said, "Riverside Campus."

For me, the name elicited visions of a serene academic enclave nestled against a gently flowing waterway, something akin to the location of Baylor University's McLane Stadium along the banks of the same Brazos River, which also flows near what is now RELLIS.

Don't fault me for my newcomer's ignorance. No less an authority than John Sharp, chancellor of the Texas A&M University System and the visionary behind the RELLIS Campus concept, said he knew nothing of the Riverside Campus—nor the Research Annex, nor even Bryan Air Force Base, names by which the location had been previously known—until he assumed his current position in 2011.

And Sharp knows much about Aggie lore. He was president of the A&M student body as a member of the Class of '72.

Beginning in 1962, Texas A&M spent two decades leasing the old Bryan Air Force Base site and another five years as outright owner before school officials realized more could be done with the former military installation.

The name change to Riverside Campus in 1988 came as part of a concerted effort to breathe new life into the 2,000-acre property. A comprehensive master plan was created, a plan that addressed a number of issues that had come to plague the venue.

"For approximately 25 years the former Bryan Air Force Base has served Texas A&M University as a location for research and extension activities," read the Purpose of Study section of the Riverside Campus Master Plan, a nearly 100-page document containing the recommendations of Bovay Engineers; Smith Lock Asakura, Inc.; The Hardin Group; and Roscoe H. Jones, Consultant.

The authors of the plan pulled no punches in assessing the venue's shortcomings.

"The former Air Force Base is burdened with an image problem, a seemingly remote location and an unattractive appearance.

"The 'Annex' is a place where few go, and then only out of necessity."

Jerry Gaston served as chairman of the Riverside Campus Master Plan steering committee. He also held the post of associate provost at Texas A&M and was deputy chancellor of the Texas A&M University System.

"For 13 years I was chairman of the Campus Facilities Planning Committee," said Gaston, who still calls Bryan home. "It was in that capacity that I headed up work on the Riverside Campus Master Plan.

"It was no secret the Research Annex was in need of sprucing up," Gaston continued. "Even after 25 years of university control, it still gave the appearance of an old Air Force base."

In 1987, the enrollment of the A&M flagship campus was about 40,000 students, and, according to the Texas Higher Education Coordinating Board, the school was about a million square feet short of its educational and general (E&G) space requirements.

"That was determined by a complicated formula based in part on the number of faculty, students, and classrooms on campus," Gaston said.

"Our board of regents asked us if the Research Annex might be a solution to our E&G shortfall, so we decided to take a look."

As Gaston remembers, the cost to produce the master plan was in the neighborhood of $200,000. Then A&M president Frank Vandiver was quick to approve the expenditure.

The study took approximately 10 months.

As founder of the Texas A&M Center for Heritage Conservation and a professor emeritus of the A&M College of Architecture, David Woodcock knows the Riverside Campus Master Plan well.

In fact, he helped put together an updated plan in 2013.

I had the privilege of giving the two longtime friends a tour of the RELLIS Campus in the summer of 2018. Road reconstruction was ongoing and new buildings were springing up in multiple locations.

Both men saw evidence of the Riverside plans in the development of the RELLIS Campus.

"The original Riverside Campus plan was typical of the 1980s in that it had wide, tree-lined roadways," Woodcock said. "It also assumed that the redevelopment of the location would start from scratch.

"The military heritage in that plan was evident only in the road patterns. Basically all the buildings would be new."

Weaving through an ever-changing maze of detours that have transformed the RELLIS Campus, the two "master planners" and I made our way along widened roadways and past new buildings onto the older, southern side of the grounds.

The long-time road configuration at the former Bryan Air Force Base has been slightly reconfigured in the RELLIS redevelopment of the site. Photo by author.

Near the intersection of 6th Street and Avenue B, Woodcock pointed out the only two barracks remaining on the site. Both housed enlisted men during World War II and the Korean War. Both were converted into storage facilities for later university use.

And both have long since been abandoned.

According to Woodcock, had the '88 plan been implemented, the barracks and most of the other historic structures that remain on the site today would have been razed long ago.

Now those buildings, many of which are along the old flight line, serve as a link to the locale's remarkable legacy.

"Thirty years ago, the university was not sure of the future of this particular institution," Woodcock said, "so, the '88 plan suggested things like a beef center, a conference center, and a golf course."

According to Gaston, there was never an earnest intent to execute the Riverside Campus Master Plan, at least in the near term. The flagship always had other pressing needs.

"The plan was intended to be a guide toward possible future development of the location," Gaston said.

That vision is now being realized.

Today, a conference center, contained within the Center for Infrastructure Renewal building, is in place at RELLIS. Other new structures include a classroom building for Blinn College, a new headquarters for the Texas A&M Transportation Institute, and a new building to serve as the home for the A&M System's "Academic Alliance" at RELLIS. The future headquarters of the Texas A&M Engineering Experiment Station will also be located on the RELLIS Campus in the years to come.

"I'm impressed with how the new vision is coming together," Woodcock said after our visit to the campus. "I believe they have successfully preserved the heritage of the place."

"It's a miracle what they're doing to the campus," Gaston added after making his first trip in almost 20 years to the former Riverside Campus. "I'm astonished."

Both men presume the Riverside Campus name stemmed from the site's proximity to the Brazos River.

That's an easy assumption to make.

The street signs at intersections along the roughly 6-mile stretch that constitutes Highway 47 to the RELLIS Campus still proclaim "Riverside Parkway." Yet, that name has nothing to do with either the river or the Riverside Campus.

A long-standing unincorporated community called Riverside, occupied mostly by immigrant cotton farmers living west of Bryan, once sat about a mile north of the banks of the Brazos River.

Riverside Parkway, officially established shortly after the Riverside Campus name gave way to RELLIS in 2016, honors the township that was eradicated for the construction of Bryan Army Air Field at the outset of World War II.

The move was a small gesture spearheaded by local historians but one that commemorates a nearly forgotten yet important piece of both local and RELLIS Campus history.

Jerry Gaston, left, former chairman of the Texas A&M Campus Facilities Planning Committee, and David Woodstock, founder of the Texas A&M Center for Heritage Conservation, stand between the last two World War II–era barracks at the RELLIS Campus. Photo by author.

Gaston and Woodcock in front of the Blinn College Schwartz Classroom Building at the RELLIS Campus. Photo by author.

Matthew Bizzell

As a Texas A&M senior majoring in both English and philosophy, Matthew Bizzell, Class of 2014, was looking for an extracurricular assignment on campus to bring his undergraduate years as an Aggie to a satisfying close. He hoped that whatever he found would, at the same time, prepare him for future studies in literature and history.

The task he found was to help tell the story of his *alma mater*.

Secrets of the Past

"It was May 2014. I was 22, and I thought I needed a job that reflected the virtues of my budding graduate career. Cushing Memorial Library was hiring a researcher for the "Mapping Historic Aggieland" project. It seemed perfect. I had actually grown up in a library, wandering through the stacks for hours a day while my sister practiced gymnastics next door.

"I had no way of knowing that the job would so closely connect with my adolescent 'perambulations.'

"I think my interview for the job was decided when they asked me about my name. 'Bizzell? Like the street?' Yes. I share that name with an uncle with a few 'greats' tacked on, at least from my place in the family tree: former Texas A&M president William Bennett Bizzell.

"Maybe it's hard not to hire a researcher with a slice of A&M history in their personal background.

"Riverside Campus was my first assignment. I was tasked with dredging up the history of the place. I was excited. Very little research had been done on Riverside, and I reveled in the opportunity. That feeling lasted until my first trip to the Cushing Library Reading Room, where I was presented the one box of surviving materials and told that a lot had been lost in a fire some decades ago. Despite being the only one of its kind, the box was optimistically labeled, 'Riverside Campus Materials Box 1,' as if more were sure to follow if only I could decipher the contents at hand.

"Every day for the next three months, I walked, with a heavy jacket in hand, through the blindingly white heat of a the Central Texas summer. The library was kept at something like 60 degrees for preservation purposes, and after four hours in the reading room, it was hard not to think of the place as some erudite arctic cave.

"In that cave, I hunted down the scraps of history that had the potential to tell the stories of the past. I sifted that lonely box and braved the unprocessed stacks for anything that could be linked to Riverside. I searched book indexes and found table-sized maps. I built Excel spreadsheets and crafted Word documents.

Matthew Bizzell *is an instructor at San Jacinto Community College in Houston. He is in pursuit of his PhD in literature and history from the University of Houston. While obtaining his dual bachelor of Arts degrees in English/creative writing and philosophy at Texas A&M, he enlisted to participate in the Cushing Memorial Library's "Mapping Historic Aggieland" project. In that role, he did extensive historical work on what was known at the time as the Riverside Campus. He went on to earn his master's degree from A&M in American literature. Matt is married and originally from San Antonio.*

Courtesy of Matthew Bizzell.

"I was determined to unlock the secrets of the past. It didn't take long for me to grow attached to this 'Riverside' place, a locale of many and conflicting identities, a nebulous collection of institutions and initiatives.

"Remarkably, at least through the hindsight of the years which have passed, I never thought to actually visit the Riverside Campus in person, at least not until I was nearly finished with the project.

"Late one Friday afternoon while working on the project, I headed home to San Antonio. On my way out of town, I noticed something that I'd passed many times before but paid no real attention to: a cluster of buildings located near the intersection of Highways 21 and 47. Immediately, I pulled over.

"'The Riverside Campus.'

"When I got out of my car, I stared at the site. Sure enough, just as I'd seen in maps of the original Bryan Army Air Field, there were large white buildings in the distance: World War II-era airplane hangars.

"I pulled onto the property grounds. There were barracks, dilapidated and unrestored. There were hangars from which pilots had flown to prepare to fight two wars. There, before me in physical form, was almost everything I had spent the summer noting, organizing, and documenting.

"I had discovered the Riverside Campus for myself that summer leafing through the pages of history. And, given all the time I had spent to learn about the place, I felt like I had reconnected with a long-lost friend."

Kyle McNew (*left*) and his father, Dr. Lamar McNew, stand in front of the TEEX Law Enforcement Building on the RELLIS Campus. Photo by author.

CHAPTER 17
Generations

The Texas A&M Engineering Extension Service—more commonly known as TEEX—offers more than 200 courses in its Law Enforcement and Security Training Division on the RELLIS Campus.

A segment of the curricula serves as "police academy" for both city and county constabulary across Texas.

Kyle McNew became a police officer through TEEX. He paid for academy training out of his own pocket.

Today, McNew is a law-enforcement training manager with that same Texas A&M University System agency. He joined the TEEX staff in 2001.

He calls TEEX "home" and credits his police-academy training for helping him turn his life around.

He's also the third generation of his family to teach.

And the third generation with ties to the RELLIS Campus.

Kyle's father, Lamar, was a prominent local physician who mentored Texas A&M premed students for decades.

Kyle's grandfather, J. T. L. McNew, was an A&M civil engineering professor and department head who ultimately became a vice president for the engineering school.

J. T. L. McNew also was namesake for the College of Engineering's McNew Materials and Structural Mechanics Laboratory, opened in 1969.

J. T. L. McNew, the eldest of three generations with ties to RELLIS. Courtesy of Kyle McNew.

Lamar McNew as an Air Force pilot. Courtesy of Kyle McNew.

Kyle McNew as a law enforcement officer with the Montgomery County Sheriff's Department. Courtesy of Kyle McNew.

With that distinguished pedigree and a young wife to support, a then-25-year-old Kyle McNew realized his destiny was to do more than blue-collar labor.

A year after graduating from Bryan High School in 1980, McNew dropped out of college. He bounced between construction jobs until landing a position as a maintenance technician with the Texas Department of Transportation.

Then, in 1986, he decided to chart a different course for his life, one influenced by a role model outside the family circle.

He opted to become a cop.

"Growing up as a kid, I looked at Bob Wiatt as *the* tough guy," McNew said recently from his office located on the RELLIS Campus in the building adjacent to the Robert E. "Bob" Wiatt Physical Skills Training Complex.

Bob Wiatt is a legendary local lawman. His son, Jeff, was one of Kyle's closest friends growing up.

"Whenever I was at Jeff's house and Bob would come home from work, he'd head straight for the garage and lift weights for a couple hours. He'd come out dripping with sweat and then go for a long run.

"I was scared to death of the guy."

As an FBI agent, Bob Wiatt's daring rescue of a kidnapped Texas Highway Patrol officer was the inspiration for Steven Spielberg's first major motion picture, *Sugarland Express*.

Later, Wiatt spent more than two decades as director of security for the Texas A&M University Police Department.

"Bob's real-life crime-fighting stories fascinated me when I was young," McNew said. "I remember thinking at the time, 'Maybe I want to be a part of that.'"

McNew's police-academy training covered a 14-week span.

"That was a challenging experience for me," McNew said. "I was trying to survive without a steady income, go to school eight hours a day, and study to pass the state licensing exam."

Upon graduation, McNew went to work with the Navasota Police Department. Fifteen years later, he left the Montgomery County Sheriff's Office to become a TEEX instructor.

McNew quickly realized that, without a college degree, his prospects for agency advancement were limited.

Thus, while serving as a TEEX trainer, McNew earned his associate's degree in criminal justice from Blinn College. He obtained a bachelor's degree in criminal justice administration from Tarleton State in 2013.

In carrying on the McNew family's teaching tradition, Kyle still lacked one important thing.

An Aggie Class Ring.

John Thomas Lamar McNew, Kyle's grandfather, was a member of the A&M Class of 1918. Following graduation, he served with the US Army in World War I.

J. T. L. McNew joined the A&M faculty in 1922 as an instructor in civil engineering. After becoming department head in 1941, he was recruited to join the Army's Corps of Engineers in 1943 for a highly classified mission: the construction of secret American bomber bases in Indochina.

McNew succeeded in that task and left the Army as a lieutenant colonel. He returned to A&M in 1944 as a vice president, a position he held for just two years when on December 21, 1946, he died following a massive cerebral hemorrhage at the age of 51.

J. T. L. McNew II, known to the family as Lamar, followed in his father's footsteps and obtained a degree in civil engineering from A&M as a member of the Class of '53.

As a freshman manager for the Aggie football team, Lamar avoided assignment to "The Annex," A&M's infamous home for first-year cadets on the site of Bryan Army Air Field from 1946 to 1950.

Members of the athletic department lived on the main campus.

Lamar did spend time on today's RELLIS Campus site after it was reactivated as Bryan Air Force Base in 1951. A civil engineering undergrad, he helped survey the first of two 7,000-foot runways added to the base to accommodate jet aircraft.

Later, as an Air Force instructor pilot himself, McNew sometimes commanded training flights from his post in Laredo back to Bryan Air Force Base where he landed on the runways he'd helped build.

It was in the Air Force that Lamar McNew decided to become a doctor.

Now retired from a Bryan-based family practice in which he spent more than 50 years, Dr. McNew, 86, still calls the area his home.

Kyle McNew's mother, Liz, also pursued a teaching career. She received her bachelor's degree in education from the University of Texas in 1957.

Then, after raising daughter Saralyn and sons Kyle and Loc, Liz went back to school, earning a master's in education from A&M in 1991. She obtained her PhD at Texas A&M in 1995 . . . at the age of 62.

Liz died in 2016 and just missed seeing Kyle receive his own master's degree in education and resource development from Texas A&M.

Kyle wears his Aggie ring proudly. It took him 55 years to get it.

Kyle McNew never knew his grandfather. J. T. L. died when his own son, Lamar, was just 14 years old.

J. T. L. McNew's legacy lived on through the McNew Laboratory, located on the A&M main campus. Under the authority of the Texas A&M Transportation Institute, the lab became one of the nation's leading roadway materials testing facilities.

But, now it's gone.

The facility was recently demolished to make way for the new Zachry Engineering Education Complex.

The research previously conducted at the McNew Laboratory has been moved . . . to the RELLIS Campus.

The new Center for Infrastructure Renewal, a collaboration between the Texas A&M Engineering Experiment Station and the Texas A&M Transportation Institute, houses a number of state-of-the-art research facilities.

One of these is the Asphalt Innovation Lab, which will advance the work previously conducted at the McNew Laboratory—bringing the spirit, if you will, of yet another generation of McNew onto the RELLIS Campus.

Perhaps someday a lab there will again carry the McNew name.

Tom Turbiville

Tom Turbiville was one of the Brazos Valley's most popular radio personalities at WTAW. He also created, produced, and hosted "Veterans of the Valley," a respected KAMU-TV series saluting service veterans from the Bryan-College Station area.

Today Tom is the radio voice of the Texas A&M women's basketball team, and as good a guy as you'll find. With tongue firmly placed in cheek, such though, has not always been the case. Several years ago at the Riverside Campus—now the RELLIS Campus—Tom took on the role of a "villain."

Hostage "Crisis"

"I was an on-air guy doing the morning show and after I got off the air I had a message from the assistant police chief of the Bryan PD. Nobody likes to get a message like that, right? So I give him a call. Fortunately, they weren't after me. Instead, he said they wanted me for something 'interesting.' They were going to be doing a mock hostage drill, a SWAT drill with all of the elements of local law enforcement—Bryan-College Station PD, University PD, and the sheriff's office. All were getting together for training on what to do in a hostage situation. This was going to happen at the Riverside Campus, the old Bryan Army Air Field.

"I said, 'Great! What part am I going to play?'

"'We thought that you would be good to be the bad guy.'

"I didn't know how to take that, but after giving it some thought, I said, 'Okay, sounds like fun.'

"Fast forward to the day of the exercise and they say that I can do anything I want. They're not going to try to influence the mind of a bad guy because I'm the person who's taking these hostages and I'm the one who has the armaments. They give me a rifle. They gave me a gun—neither had real ammunition—and they say, 'Okay, you're going to take a family hostage in this house. And it turns out this 'house' was an old officer's quarters, a house in a string of small homes out there at the time. And the only way I remember which home it was (was that) it had a big tree in the front yard."

(Planted there by the Air Force squad commander father of John A. Adams.)

"Now this tree's going to come into the story in a little bit.

Tom Turbiville *is the play-by-play voice of the Texas A&M University women's basketball team. He's also a well-known and well-regarded former local-market radio and television personality. He co-hosted the WTAW "Infomaniacs" morning show for 19 years and created and hosted the "Veterans of the Valley" series on Texas A&M's PBS affiliate, KAMU-TV. Prior to his broadcasting career, Turbiville was sports editor of the Irving Daily News, assistant media relations director for the Southwest Conference, and sports information director at Texas A&M.*

Courtesy of Tom Turbiville.

"So we begin the drill and they put me in the house.

"The hostages are there and they say 'Action!' just like in the movies, and we get started. All of a sudden I'm surrounded by law enforcement officers outside and they're yelling at me with the bull horns. One of the officers makes his way up and hides behind that big tree and I can see him. So I figured he's the guy that's going to come in with guns blazing to try to stop this situation because I'm the bad guy. And I say to myself, 'Okay, they said I could do anything I wanted to do.' So, I had an idea. I could run out the front door with my gun, go and take that guy and put my arm around his neck and bring him back into the house and hold him hostage.'

"So I do. I go out and take him by the neck and back up. I've got the gun to his head—you know, I'm just all like *Gunsmoke*—and I take him into the house. I'm holding *him* hostage. I take his two-way radio and I start talking to the guys on the other end, saying, 'I've got your officer and I've got the two-way radio and you all back off or I'm going to kill one hostage every 30 minutes,.' It's like total 'Hollywood.' They weren't ready for that at all.

"Eventually, though, they get the bad guy.

"They finally surrounded me. I'm caught. They have me. They come in the back door, in through the kitchen. They say, 'Get on your stomach! Get on your hands and knees! Spread them!!!' Now they've got me thinking maybe I really am a bad guy. They arrest me, slapping on the handcuffs, and the hostage situation is negated.

"So they did their part. I did my part, and that's my main memory of the old Riverside Campus."

Dr. Juliana Rangel (*right*) and graduate student Liz Walsh study a bee frame behind the Texas A&M Honey Bee Facility on the RELLIS Campus. Photo by author.

CHAPTER 18

Baboons, Bovines, and Bees

In the spring of 2018, a feisty group of San Antonians made national headlines after going on a seemingly innocuous field trip from their home.

The curiosity-seekers were baboons, four of which had escaped from the Texas Biomedical Research Institute after rolling a 55-gallon barrel to the wall of their enclosure, standing it upright, and then climbing out to freedom.

The primates went on a brief walkabout before being captured and safely returned to the center.

Research baboons have been cared for at the facility for more than 50 years.

Their descendants lived for a time just west of Bryan at what today is called the RELLIS Campus.

According to the Third Annual Report of the Texas A&M Research Annex, filed with the Department of Health, Education and Welfare and prepared by Texas A&M University in its "lease-to-own" arrangement for the Annex property, eight baboons were a part of the animal population at the old Bryan Air Force Base in 1965.

The report outlined the "Anatomical and Physiological Studies of the Baboon," which sought "to establish normals for further studies involving the baboon as a laboratory animal for research."

Two years earlier, in 1963, the Southwestern Foundation for Research and Education held the International Symposium on the Baboon in San Antonio.

As a result of that conference, small baboon colonies sprung up in a variety of places, including the Texas A&M Research Annex.

After a year of study, A&M scientists published *An Atlas of the Anatomy of the Baboon.*

Dr. Duane Kraemer was a Texas A&M student in the mid-1960s, pursuing both PhD and doctor of veterinary medicine degrees. Later, while working at the Southwestern Foundation, he specialized in "contraceptive agents and embryo transfer" in baboons.

"I wasn't a part of that original study at the Research Annex," Kraemer said, "but when I came back to Texas A&M as a researcher, I did work with a small group of baboons on the main campus.

"Through the years, baboon studies have been critical in creating medical advances in humans, including in the fields of heart disease, osteoporosis, and epilepsy."

In addition to his work with baboons, Kraemer was also a part of the Texas A&M scientific team that produced the world's first cloned cat in December 2001. "CC," as she was named, followed Kramer into retirement in the Bryan-College Station area and late in 2018 celebrated her 17th birthday.

The Foundation of Applied Research was started in 1941 by the late San Antonio oilman and Texas A&M benefactor Thomas Slick, Jr.

Today the foundation is known as the Texas Biomedical Research Institute, and its work with baboons continues.

While primates no longer populate the RELLIS Campus, other animals still can be found there today. Pens and a small pasture near the north end of the air base's old flight line contain cattle involved in an A&M AgriLife husbandry research study.

Livestock have long been a fixture at RELLIS.

And where there are farm animals, fences usually can be found. One of Texas A&M's most respected former administrators knows all about that.

Larry Boleman grew up on a farm in McLennan County, Texas. His ability to attend Texas A&M as a student hinged on a scholarship he received from the Waco A&M Mothers' Club in 1964.

When those funds ran out, young Larry was forced to find a job.

The job he found was with the Texas A&M Beef Cattle Center.

"Back when I was a student, the Beef Cattle Center was on what today is the West Campus," said Boleman, the recently retired associate vice chancellor for the Texas A&M AgriLife Extension Service. "That land was then occupied by all the 'farms' of the agriculture school: cattle, horses, swine, poultry, and horticulture."

The Texas A&M Research Annex's nearly 2,000 acres offered an opportunity for expansion close to the main campus. A decision was made to run a portion of the university's cattle herd there.

Dr. Larry Boleman, former associate vice chancellor for the Texas A&M AgriLife Extension Service, stands in a livestock pen on the RELLIS Campus. Boleman helped erect fencing at the former Texas A&M Research Annex in the mid-1960s. Photo by author.

Thus there was a need to build miles and miles of fences.

"And it was hot," Boleman recalled of his summer of 1965. "The process was pretty low-tech. We took a post-hole digger, dug out the dirt, put in a pole, and stretched the wire."

Boleman looks back on the early days of the Research Annex and marvels at how A&M was able to make innovative use of the old military base.

The world's first college-based feedlot management program began there.

"Dr. Lowell Schake headed up that effort in the early '70s," Boleman said. "He took one end of an old runway, put up panels and shade, laid down dirt, brought in water, and created a series of miniature feedlots for his students to oversee."

At about the same time, in 1974, the Parsons Mounted Cavalry got its start on a five-acre plot of land at the Research Annex, reviving a Corps of Cadets' tradition that ended with the onset of World War II.

Combat horsemanship had been a part of A&M's original military instruction when the school first opened in 1876, and a cavalry detachment endured on campus until 1943.

The Parsons unit remained on the RELLIS site for only a couple years. The detail then moved to its present location at Fiddler's Green, on the corner of Harvey Mitchell Parkway and F&B Road just west of the main campus.

The most intriguing non-human occupants on today's RELLIS Campus are *Apis mellifera*, otherwise known as the western honey bee.

The Janice and John G. Thomas Honey Bee Facility sits on the east side of RELLIS, away from the "buzz" of redevelopment activity ongoing at the location.

According to Dr. Juliana Rangel, the Honey Bee Lab's director, new neighbors need not concern themselves with the approximately 2 million bees she and her staff oversee.

"We don't typically have any issues," Rangel said. "Our bees are quite gentle."

Typically.

"Every now and then we have an aggressive colony," she admitted, "but we try to manage them by killing the queen, because she is the one producing the aggressive workers."

Bee entomology is a fascinating field. A queen lays as many as 2,000 eggs a day. Fertilized eggs hatch into female worker bees. Unfertilized eggs become drones, the males of a colony.

The bees you see hovering around plant life outside your home are worker bees completing tasks that mark the end of their four- to five-month lifespans.

Thanks in part to research being done at RELLIS, the "colony collapse disorder" crisis that threatened the global bee population for several years has dissipated. Scientists now realize that insecticides previously used by apiculturists to eradicate the pestilent varroa mite were often toxic to the bees themselves.

Keeping Texas beekeepers educated and informed is a component of the work done by Rangel and her team.

On the sweeter side of the A&M bee story, Rosenthal's Meat Science and Technology Center is again stocking Aggie Honey after a more than two-year absence.

The honey comes from the Honey Bee Lab.

A Brazos Valley breakfast biscuit's tastiest topping is a byproduct of the research work being done today on the RELLIS Campus.

Jars of honey from the RELLIS Campus. Photo by author.

Jorge Vanegas

__Dr. Jorge Vanegas__ began serving as dean of the Texas A&M College of Architecture in 2008. He has been a technical advisor and a regular contributor to activities of different academic institutions, organizations, and companies in the United States and internationally and serves on boards for several research and education centers. In recognition of his scholarly accomplishments in research, teaching, and service, Dr. Vanegas has received national and international awards for education, research, and professional excellence, including being inducted into the Pan American Academy of Engineering in 2010. A registered architect in his home country of Colombia, Dr. Vanegas holds a degree in architecture from Universidad de los Andes in Bogotá.

Courtesy of Texas A&M College of Architecture.

The Automated Fabrication & Design Lab—known since its inception in 2008 as the "Architectural Ranch"—is the Texas A&M College of Architecture's large-scale research and fabrication facility located on the RELLIS Campus.

It is dedicated to the advancement of student, faculty, and industry projects. The lab utilizes the latest industry and research-driven technologies to provide a "hands-on" learning environment for students. It also provides complete project fabrication and engineering services for all colleges within the university and for outside clientele as well.

Dr. Jorge Vanegas is dean of the A&M College of Architecture.

The Architectural Ranch

"This facility is a very unique facility for a college of architecture. A lot of people outside Texas A&M don't realize that when you use the word "architecture," it is not just the Department of Architecture. It's actually the college and that includes specialties in urban planning, landscape architecture, construction science, and visualization.

"This is a facility that actually serves the complete college, not just architecture. Its original title, said very affectionately, was the 'Architectural Ranch,' and its initial conception was to provide an extension to where architecture is on campus, which is the Langford Architecture Center complex with three buildings. So when this facility was conceived, it was an extension of the learning environment that you have in a normal classroom, in a normal design studio, in a normal laboratory, where students could actually play hands-on with their designs.

"In 2008, when we created this facility at the Riverside Campus—now the RELLIS Campus—we had 16 acres, and in those 16 acres, we had land to actually create demonstrations and pilot projects that integrate all the disciplines of architecture. One of the big initial projects was our participation in the National Solar Decathlon. The facility (we built) was a fully operational house completely off the grid that was built here, transported to Washington and assembled there, then transported back to campus. And it spent a year at the Bush Library.

"In addition, this is a facility that has helped build 'tiny houses' that are actually being used for veterans. We have supported the construction of 'tiny clinics,' which spun off from the tiny houses, that provide examination rooms and treatment rooms for disadvantaged communities. So this facility is a catalyst for innovation. And that transcends the college environment.

"At any given moment in time, you could have seen in this facility elements that have been created working together with nautical archeology. We have been creating a testbed in the use of drones, unmanned vehicles for inspection of roofs after storms or any kind of an extreme weather event. We have helped create mechanisms to clean up dogs that participate in rescue missions so that they can be decontaminated. We have worked with artists who need space to unleash their creative juices.

"If you look around, this looks like a warehouse. If you look around, it's a metal building with a roof. But this is a facility that defies a stereotype or defies any type of typical taxonomy for a building. What matters is that this is a place where dreams actually can materialize for students as part of the transformational learning that occurs in many of the programs in our college."

Building 7046, the old Bryan Army Air Field World War II Transient Aircraft hangar, next to the Korean War–era flight control tower on today's RELLIS Campus. Photo by author.

CHAPTER 19
Final Flights

While the RELLIS Campus flight control tower stands abandoned now, it remains a monument to the extraordinary history of its surroundings.

Once catalyst to the rumble and roar of a seemingly endless line of military aircraft soaring into the Central Texas sky, the old lookout bears witness today to the blare and bellow of construction equipment reconfiguring the local landscape.

Nearby sits another historic structure, a World War II–era hangar known today as Building 7046.

More than a half century ago, that same hanger, under the auspices of Texas A&M University, housed the prototypes of what would become the world's most widely used aircraft devoted to agriculture: the Grumman G-164 Ag Cat.

That plane spawned the US Department of Agriculture's Aerial Application Technology research group at A&M's Research Annex.

Fred Bouse, then a young USDA agricultural engineer, arrived in College Station in 1964.

His first job with the Agriculture Research Service (ARS) was in Stillwater, Oklahoma, where he had received bachelor's and master's degrees from Oklahoma A&M College.

"My assignment here at Texas A&M was to help conduct research on the defoliation of woody vegetation," Bouse said recently.

He retired from the USDA in 1994 and still lives in the local area.

"By the time I got here," he continued, "ARS weed-science personnel had already started a woody-plant nursery between the runways at the Research Annex.

"It became our job to figure out how to kill those trees."

The project to which Bouse was assigned was funded by the Defense Advanced Research Projects Agency (DARPA). The mission was to find an herbicide to reduce the dense jungle vegetation hampering the US war effort in Vietnam.

There were two elements to the project: concocting the most effective chemical formula to achieve the desired result, and testing the aerial application profile of delivery mechanisms.

Lab work was done in numerous locations across the country, including on A&M's main campus.

Flight testing originated at the former Bryan Air Force Base.

All Bouse's team needed was a plane to fly.

"Joe Brusse, a researcher in A&M's aeronautical engineering department, informed me that the 'X-1' model of Grumman's original agricultural aircraft was located in one of the wooden hangars at the Research Annex."

Grumman had donated to A&M both their 'X-1' and 'X-2' versions of the Ag Cat—a biplane—after Brusse had designed and successfully tested optimal spray-nozzle configurations for the aircraft.

"The 'X-2' model was disassembled and crated," Bouse said. "The 'X-1,' though intact, hadn't been flown for several years."

Bouse's ARS team refurbished the plane and used it to conduct local field studies—some on the grounds of the Research Annex site—pertaining to the penetration of spray-through foliage canopies, as well as the effectiveness of the various herbicides being tested for the DARPA project.

"Research by the ARS team resulted in the selection of a compound which was packaged in orange-striped barrels," Bouse said.

In those barrels was the herbicidal stew that became infamously known as "Agent Orange."

"It was a one-to-one mixture of '2,4,5-T,' which had proven effective in controlling mesquite growth in Texas," Bouse said, "and '2,4-D,' which is still used today for weed control in people's yards."

The first military application of the compound that would later come to be known as Agent Orange occurred during the Malayan Emergency in the early 1950s. The British used a similar mix to eradicate jungle vegetation and impact the enemy's food supply in a successful effort to turn back a communist insurrection that took place within the Federation of Malaya.

Between 1962 and 1971, as part of "Project Ranch Hand," the US military unleashed a series of "Rainbow Herbicides" in other areas of Southeast Asia.

Agents "Green," "Pink," "Purple," and "Blue" were used prior to Agent Orange's refinement through the USDA's ARS program.

More than 20 million gallons of tactical herbicide were disseminated during the Vietnam War. "At concentrations 20 to 55 times the agricultural use rate of the time," Bouse added.

Agent Orange proved effective as a defoliant . . . and toxic to humans.

As many as 3 million Vietnamese purportedly suffered illnesses because of exposure to Agent Orange during the war in Southeast Asia. US military personnel there suffered too. But for many years, the official record suggested otherwise.

Only after an arduous and decades-long debate over the harmful effects of Agent Orange did the US Department of Veteran Affairs start providing medical care and disability compensation to service personnel for Agent Orange-related illnesses . . . beginning in 2015.

In the years following the tactical herbicide project, the USDA's local Aerial Application Technology (AAT) group has used the old Bryan Field runways to spearhead a number of important advances in the efficiency and safety of applying crop-protection chemicals from aircraft.

Lee Denham has worked full-time with the USDA's local AAT program since 2006.

The title on his business card reads, simply, "Pilot."

While A&M's aging Grumman Ag Cat served Denham's predecessors well, the AAT had as many as four aircraft of its own hangared at the south end of the flight line on the Riverside and RELLIS Campuses over the last decade.

During that time, Denham was the only person authorized to fly in and out of the RELLIS site.

"On research missions, I flew about 50 hours a year," Denham said.

Flight directives were determined by USDA scientists.

"Some of our research was actually done on flights over RELLIS," Denham said, "spraying mostly water and florescent dyes on runways to determine parameters like nozzle placement, droplet size, uniformity, and drift, all of which comprise the science of 'crop dusting.'

"We also flew extensively throughout Texas taking photographs, which were used in our research."

But flights from RELLIS are now a thing of the past.

With college students today occupying a portion of the grounds

Lee Denham (holding helmet) and the USDA Aerial Application Technology team pose with aircraft at the RELLIS Campus. Courtesy of the US Department of Agriculture.

at the RELLIS Campus—albeit a good distance from the runway complex there—the USDA ART program was forced to abandon its operations and seek a more secure location.

Its new home is the City of Bryan's Coulter Field.

As for RELLIS, three "final flights" took place there in the summer of 2017 as the USDA ferried its fleet of planes off the site.

On July 28, Denham flew the USDA's Cessna 206 to Brenham Municipal Airport, the AAT's temporary home.

Three days later, on July 31, a bright yellow Air Tractor AT402B bid farewell to its long-time home.

And then, on August 11, 2017, Denham climbed into the cockpit of the AAT's Robinson R-44 helicopter.

After running through his preliminary flight check, he grabbed the collective and cyclic controls, opened the throttle, and slowly lifted the craft off the ground.

Once airborne, he banked to the southwest and left RELLIS for the final time.

"I know the history of this place and that history means a lot to me," Denham said of RELLIS's aviation legacy.

His final flights marked the end of a nearly 75-year-long local aviation era.

USAD flight testing, in an Air Tractor AT402B, over the runways of the RELLIS Campus. USDA aircraft were the last to fly in and out of the former Bryan Air Force Base. Courtesy of the US Department of Agriculture.

Center for Infrastructure Renewal

The need to develop solutions for infrastructure renewal was recognized by the Texas Legislature in 2015 when it authorized the construction of the Center for Infrastructure Renewal (CIR), a joint center between two renowned Texas A&M University System agencies: the Texas A&M Engineering Experiment Station (TEES) and the Texas A&M Transportation Institute (TTI).

The CIR is a state-of-the-art research center—and the first of numerous new buildings on the redeveloped RELLIS Campus—that develops transformative infrastructure solutions. The Center provides the facilities and the multidisciplinary research environments to attract significant cross-industry and government agency participation. In addition, it seeks to educate the 21st-century workforce needed to build and operate this new infrastructure.

Dr. Zachary Grasley heads up the CIR.

"A Great Spot To Be"

"The Center for Infrastructure Renewal is a facility focused on transforming civil infrastructure in the United States and beyond. The RELLIS Campus presents a great opportunity to essentially rethink how we're doing research and developing research that can be translated very rapidly into practice. It is, in essence, a big blank slate, and it allows for lots of opportunities that just don't exist on other campuses throughout the country.

"Infrastructure with respect to how we view it in the Center for Infrastructure Renewal is quite broad. Obviously there's a big transportation component with TTI and its immense presence on this campus and in the center, but (the work) goes well beyond that. We're sitting right now in a control center that houses the Smart-Grid Center that focuses on the electrical grid and research and training associated with the electrical grid throughout the United States. We also have a corrosion lab in the facility. We do work on buildings and transportation-related stuff that is quite obvious when it comes to infrastructure.

"This facility is almost 140,000 square feet in size and cost about $80 million, largely paid for by the State of Texas. I've been in a lot of infrastructure research labs around the country and I've never seen anything quite like this. We also have the training facility attached to all of these labs. That training facility is also very unique and gives us the opportunity to take the new technologies that we develop, the new innovations, and actually translate them into practice.

"I like to call our facility the 'flagship building' of RELLIS. Over the years this has been a great location where, for instance, you could do outdoor-exposure sites. You could build things that are very large, too big to build in a laboratory. A full-scale bridge was built out here, still sitting on the property.

"It's an exciting place to be, watching all the growth and construction around us. This is a great big 'toy box,' more or less, and if you're somebody who just likes building things and being at the forefront of research, this is a great spot to be."

Dr. Zachary Grasley *is a renowned civil engineer whose research focuses on the integration of analytical, computational, and experimental techniques to fundamentally advance civil infrastructure materials. He serves as director of the Center for Infrastructure Renewal and is a professor and Presidential Impact Fellow in the Zachry Department of Civil Engineering at Texas A&M University. Grasley has published over 50 peer-reviewed journal articles and has given over 30 invited or keynote seminars. He is the former chair of the Cements Division of the American Ceramic Society and associate editor for the ASCE Journal of Materials in Civil Engineering.*

Courtesy of Texas A&M Engineering Experiment Station.

Blinn College District at RELLIS; Walter C. Schwartz Building. Courtesy of the Texas A&M University System. Photo by author.

CHAPTER 20

The Future of RELLIS

Gary Sera, the former agency director for the Texas A&M Engineering Extension Service, likes to tell the story of how people used to stop by his office when he worked at what was then called the Riverside Campus.

"Coming into town on State Highway 21, people would see the sign saying, 'Texas A&M Riverside,' Sera said.

He spent nearly 30 years with TEEX, becoming agency director in 2008.

"Those folks would pull in looking for someone to give them directions," he continued. "For many, Riverside was their first impression of A&M. Some thought it *was* A&M."

Sera knew the Riverside Campus offered a less-than-ideal image of what Texas A&M had become.

"Back then, most of what you saw at Riverside was mesquite trees, cows, and fences," Sera chuckled.

He decided to take things up with his boss: the newly hired chancellor of the Texas A&M University System, John Sharp.

"I remember that conversation like it was yesterday," Sharp said of his introduction to Riverside in 2011. "Gary told me the place could be something really special if we could figure out a way to use it.

"I was embarrassed by what it looked like."

Five years later the A&M System took control of Riverside. Sharp was determined to give the locale a new vision and a new life.

Others had seen the potential in the 2,000-acre property. In 1988, when the former Texas A&M Research Annex was rebranded as the Riverside Campus, a master plan commissioned for the site was presented to the A&M Board of Regents. Another Riverside master plan was executed in 2013.

In that document, then Texas A&M President R. Bowen Loftin called the Riverside Campus "arguably the (university's) most deeply rooted physical resource (at the) interconnection between quality education, research, and dedication to service."

He went on to say, "The Riverside Campus (has) contributed immensely to A&M's reputation and status in fields of key national needs." He was referring to the research and training activities of TEEX, the Texas A&M Transportation Institute, and the Texas A&M Engineering Experiment Station, also known as TEES. Each of those agencies have had a decades-long presence at what is now the RELLIS Campus.

"The Riverside Campus," Loftin concluded in his "Letter from the President," " (is) an integral part of the university, support(s) the aspiration and vision of our faculty and research leaders and recall(s) the distinguished history of service and sacrifice."

RELLIS, both the idea and the campus, has emerged more than 50 years after Texas A&M took control of the old Bryan Air Force Base installation in 1962. John Sharp made the announcement on May 1, 2016, at a TTI conference.

"We thought we knew what we wanted to do out there, but we couldn't decide when to declare a 'starting point,'" Sharp says. "Then Kathy Banks (vice chancellor and dean of the A&M College of Engineering) and Dennis Christianson (former TTI agency director) suggested I make the announcement at the TTI annual conference."

At that event, Sharp said, "We must offer new, transformative business models whether we are moving our research from the laboratories into the marketplace or helping more students to achieve a college education. RELLIS is a big idea and it's important that the Texas A&M University System nurture big ideas. It is only through big ideas like this that Texas can achieve its goals for higher education. RELLIS began with a $350 million redevelopment campaign that will establish it as "a place where new technologies are created and innovated, where leaders are educated and trained, and where ideas that transform our world are born and tested."

Kathy Banks' initial hope for the property was far more meager when she first discussed it with Sharp. "It was in terrible, terrible shape," Banks recalls. "Actually, I was asking him if he could invest a small bit of money to repair the roads, replace the sewage system, and perhaps renovate some of the buildings. Otherwise, I thought the best alternative was to abandon the land."

Instead, RELLIS today is home to, or soon will be, the headquarters for both Banks' Texas A&M Engineering Experiment Station and the Texas A&M Transportation Institute. Those two A&M System agencies have collaborated in the development, construction, and launch of the Center for Infrastructure Renewal, a research facility founded by the state.

TEES, TTI, and TEEX will continue their internationally known research and training missions at the site. Their work is expected to attract both private-sector and governmental partners to the location.

In 2019, the US Army Futures Command announced it will use the RELLIS Campus to conduct key research activities.

Research, testing, and training have a long history at RELLIS, but at the heart of the campus's legacy is education. As a military post, the site served as a training base during America's involvement in two major wars. As an extension of Texas A&M's long-standing land-grant-college mission, students have taken classes there, in subjects as diverse as nautical archaeology, electronics, architectural design and fabrication, law-enforcement training, and beekeeping.

In that same spirit, RELLIS is home to John Sharp's "Academic Alliance" too.

The Alliance is one part Blinn College, for students in their first two years of higher-education learning, and 10 parts Texas A&M University Systems schools.

When the Blinn College Schwartz Classroom Building opened on the RELLIS Campus for the fall semester of 2018, more than 1,600 students were enrolled there on a full-time basis, a remarkable number given the "pioneering" nature of the endeavor.

"Blinn's history changed forever on April 28, 2016," says the school's chancellor, Mary Helmsley. "That's when I met with Executive Vice Chairman Bill Hamilton and Vice Chancellor for Academic Affairs James Hallmark representing the A&M System. They laid out for me a vision that Chancellor John Sharp had shared with the Texas A&M Board of Regents about a concept called 'RELLIS' and I hung on their every word.

"We talked for more than an hour and focused, not on what has been in the past, but rather about the future of our respective institutions. The future for our children and their children and their children.

"When they asked me if I thought Blinn would be interested in being involved, my answer was an immediate and enthusiastic, 'Yes!'"

Most intriguing about the Academic Alliance is the interconnection of degree programs now offered at RELLIS from the A&M System schools.

DaNeetra Walker is the academic admissions coordinator for the RELLIS Campus.

"I think of the Academic Alliance as an umbrella," Walker says. "In addition to the Texas A&M main campus, there are 10 other universi-

RELLIS Campus aerial view. Courtesy of the Texas A&M University System.

ties in the A&M System. At RELLIS, we're going to offer degree programs from those 10 other schools right here in the Bryan-College Station area."

According to Walker, students who complete their first two years of study at any community college in the state now have the chance to complete a four-year degree at RELLIS with each A&M System school offering bachelor's degree programs in areas of study for which the institutions are known.

For instance, a Tarleton State degree in criminal justice is now available on the RELLIS Campus. Students interested in health sciences study can obtain a degree from West Texas A&M without leaving the Brazos Valley.

RELLIS officials admit that part of the appeal of the Academic Alliance is affording community-college graduates the opportunity to continue their education and experience an "Aggie" lifestyle without being a student at the Texas A&M flagship campus.

The Blinn-RELLIS partnership is of particular significance to John Sharp.

"Our relationship now with Blinn may be the most special between any university and community college in the country," Sharp says. "The RELLIS Academic Alliance now allows thousands of Blinn students the chance to continue their education right here at home.

"I want to be nice about this, but why would you want to go to a lesser university than the ones we have in the A&M System? Rather than packing up your stuff, leaving your friends, and moving across the state, you can continue your education right here and be a part of the A&M family, which is probably what you wanted from the beginning."

But the value of RELLIS academically doesn't stop there. According to Kathy Banks, undergraduate and graduate students from the A&M main campus benefit from the redevelopment and expansion of the RELLIS Campus, too.

"Our students take what they learn in the classroom, come out here, and test their ideas," Banks says. "Graduate students have facilities like no other to conduct their research, to publish their work from an environment where they can do continual testing."

RELLIS also has expanded its vocational and technical training mission. TEEX continues to lead in training a wide range of professional pursuits, and now Blinn College is offering training and certificate programs in fields with abundant job opportunities.

All of which is good for the local community . . . and the local economy.

Texas State Representative John Raney, a Texas A&M graduate and long-time College Station businessman, appreciates that fact.

"RELLIS is going to be a big deal, and not just here locally," Raney said. "Look at its proximity to Austin, to Dallas, and to Houston. It will attract business, industry, and research. It's got a world of potential."

Bryan Mayor Andrew Nelson agrees.

"Bryan Air Force Base was a huge part of the local community," Nelson said, "not only in the mission they had to protect our freedoms, but in the payroll that was generated and then invested here in the Brazos Valley.

"We have a state that is growing so fast and that means our educational needs are growing, too. Just like back when the site was a military post, RELLIS still serves a similar purpose, which is to scale up dramatically and get things done."

"We're building a small city," says Kelly Templin, director of the RELLIS Campus for the Texas A&M University System. "It's probably hard to imagine what this place is going to look like 20 years from now.

"When you look at the intended student presence here, you look at the research that will be done here, the interactions with the Department of Defense and Department of Energy, the work that will be done with private industry out here, I don't think anyone can fully realize the potential that exists here. I could try to draw you a picture, but it won't look like that.

"It will look better than you can imagine."

Joint Library Facility at the RELLIS Campus. Photo by author.

Gateway to RELLIS Campus. Courtesy of the Texas A&M University System.

David Chapman

David Chapman graduated from A&M in 1967 and then, after a stint in the military, returned to the school in 1972, working his way from a graduate assistant in the A&M Libraries to the position of director of the Cushing Memorial Library.

As former archivist for the university, Chapman is well aware of the history of the RELLIS Campus. While Texas A&M University System–affiliated state agencies like the Texas A&M Engineering Experiment Station, the Texas A&M Engineering Extension Service, and the Texas A&M Transportation Institute have made extensive and productive use of the RELLIS site for many years, many other departments within the flagship campus also used RELLIS . . . mostly for storage.

__David Chapman__ earned a bachelor's degree in history from Texas A&M University in 1967. He began working at the school in 1972, starting as a graduate assistant in the Libraries department. He became archivist for the school in 1994 and was named director of the Cushing Memorial Library in 2008. He retired from the school on January 30, 2012, after 38 years of university service. He remains an integral part of the local historical scene.

Photo by author.

A Treasure Found

"The university archives had materials stored out there. We were desperate for space. In that regard, nothing has changed. They put us out there and in an old building and what was interesting to me is they had an explosives, technically a 'deactivation' of explosives class, next door to the storage building. They displayed mines and all kinds of bombs outside, and it made me a little nervous. I'd talk to people and they said, 'They're not really active, they're just teaching tools,' but it gave one pause to go into our storage area.

"Our storage was World War II construction. We had air-conditioning put in because, as you might imagine, archives need to be stored in a cool area. So in the old barracks and warehouses out at Riverside is where we put just about everything.

"I went out there one day and found snake skins on some of my boxes. I thought, 'Hmm, there's a snake in here somewhere,' but never found it.

"Our stuff was out there at what is now the RELLIS Campus for a long time, until they decided they were going to demolish all of those buildings. Our artifacts, archives, and records have since been moved.

"When we were restoring the Cushing Library, we were desperate to find and restore or even recreate the iron grill work that used to mark the entrance into the Cushing Reading Room. Our maintenance manager for the library spent a lot of time at the Riverside Campus trying to find it, and one day he called me and said that he thought he had located the gate.

"My boss and I went out there in this raging thunderstorm. We got into the building and there it was. It lay on the floor in a pool of water, holding up pallets. Here's this wonderful—and priceless—work of art, made on the campus by students and depicting brands from many of Texas's most historic ranches, 'protecting' wooden pallets that you'd get five bucks a piece for.

"Because it was iron, it wasn't really damaged. We got it sandblasted and repainted and it's now the 'Class of '47 Gate,' again marking the entrance to the Cushing Reading Room.

"That's an amazing piece of Texas history.

"I think it's important to see what you can do with things. Sometimes, the use of it may not be readily apparent, and it takes time. I think now the administration of the System has decided, 'We're going to do something with this place,' and I think they're absolutely right in doing it. It's time to do something with this marvelous piece of land.

"It just kind of languished, but now we're going to make great use of it. It's going to be this magnificent project and I'm not sure they know how good it's going to be and where it's going to go. I think it's going to be far greater than anybody imagined."

Ann Burns and Arlen Crouch, just two of countless local residents whose lives were touched by activities at the site of today's RELLIS Campus. Photo by author.

EPILOGUE
Dreams Die Hard

Two of the most compelling recollections of RELLIS Campus history came as a result of an invitation I received to speak at the Arbor Oaks retirement community in Bryan.

I was familiar with Arbor Oaks. Bill and Mary Jo Lay live there, as do Dr. Duane Kraemer and his wife, Shirley.

The Arbor Oaks invite was extended by phone, from a resident there named Ann Burns. Ann initially made no mention of her own ties to RELLIS. Given her obvious excitement about the subject, Ann's offer was one I couldn't refuse. In accepting, I told her I looked forward to meeting her soon.

On the day of the event, I was welcomed by the facility's lifestyle director, Nancy Knutson. She assured me I would be speaking to an enthusiastic group.

She also offered an apology on behalf of one of her residents.

"He wanted to be here but can't make it," she said. "He did something out at the old base," Knutson said. "He mentioned something about a 'flying saucer.'"

Knutson laughed. "Does that mean anything to you?"

Her words snapped me to attention.

"I do know about the flying saucer," I told her. "I'd pretty much given up hope that I would ever meet anyone who also knew about it."

On my first trip to the Cushing Memorial Library to begin research on the RELLIS history project, I came across an old newspaper clipping from *The Bryan Daily Eagle*. The headline to the story read, "Unique Aircraft To Be Developed."

According to the spring of 1962 story, a Houston company was making plans to locate a group at the A&M Research Annex to begin work on an aircraft "which resembles a flying saucer."

The company was the Astro-Kinetic Corporation, and its product was called the "Astro-Kinetic Lift." The vehicle was a vertical takeoff and landing craft designed to fly using an aerodynamic principal called the "Coandă" effect.

A photo published in the July 1963 edition of *Popular Science* magazine reveals the Astro-Kinetic "contraption"—in this case, the word fits perfectly—one that looks remarkably like . . . a flying saucer.

Houston television station KTRH recently uncovered archival video footage of the machine. In the 15-second clip, viewable online, the company's president, Fremont Burger, can be seen with a prototype that looks like something Wile E. Coyote would have purchased from the Acme Corporation.

Before my visit to Arbor Oaks, I had learned a few details about the Astro-Kinetic Lift. Efforts to get the aircraft—and the company—off the ground commenced on July 23, 1962, when Burger's team delivered its operational prototype to what today is the Texas A&M Transportation Institute hangar along the RELLIS Campus flight line.

Burger told a small gathering of media he assembled there he hoped to have his creation airborne in as little as two months.

The Arbor Oaks resident who had knowledge of this unusual airship turned out to be Arlen Crouch, the long-time owner of Bryan Marine.

What I learned when I finally met Arlen a few weeks after my talk was that he was the reason Burger had come to town in the first place.

Crouch and friend Freddie Goehl had made a name for themselves in the 1950s as designers and builders of high-performance outboard engines. Living in Illinois, the two were speedboat enthusiasts who had achieved success on the racing circuit.

What lured Crouch and Goehl to the Lone Star State was a group of wealthy Texans intent on creating a winning speedboat-racing team themselves. They offered to bankroll a boat shop in Bryan for the two young men.

Somehow, Fremont Burger found out about Crouch's engine-building prowess and contracted with him to put an outboard engine on his aircraft, which he hoped would earn him a lucrative multimillion-dollar contract from the US Navy.

"No sooner had we got here, we were asked to help with this project," Crouch told me. "They wanted a lightweight engine that would produce a large number of RPMs to operate this 'blower fan,' or whatever they called it back then."

The vehicle, later called the "Dyna-Lift," worked on the principle of large quantities of air flowing over the inverted saucer, or "wing," of the aircraft. The Coandă affect—named for Romanian aviation pioneer Henri Coandă—bent the air down, thus creating aerodynamic lift.

Burger was betting a huge sum of money that the Astro-Kinetic lift would provide an efficient and economical means to move equipment, or even passengers, from one point to another.

Crouch recalls the "wing" of the aircraft to have been 30 to 40 feet in diameter. The rest of the initial prototype assemblage included the "blower," of a much smaller diameter than the wing, a flywheel, a seat, and four spindly legs on which the craft sat.

"The key to flight was keeping the weight to a minimum," Crouch said. "That's why they went with our outboard engine."

Crouch remembers the first attempt to gain liftoff.

"The aircraft sat on scales which could measure whether we were generating enough lift to move the vehicle, even a little. The original engine we took out there was pretty standard. We were given an operational target of so many RPMs and we exceeded that mark, but the craft didn't move."

Crouch and Goehl went back to their machine shop to find more horsepower. They bored out one of their advanced racing engines, modified it, and brought that back to the hangar.

"We were out there one night at two o'clock in the morning" Crouch explained, "and we cranked up the engine. It went way past the RPM rating they wanted, but the thing just sat there.

"At that point, they may have gone back to the drawing board, because we never saw or heard from them again."

And for nearly 50 years, that was all of the story that Arlen Crouch knew.

Ann Burns arrived for my presentation after I began to speak, and so I didn't get to meet her until after I had finished.

She is a delightful woman in her late 80s. At Arbor Oaks, she told me her late husband, Curtis Burns, had been stationed at Bryan Air Force Base early in his military career.

"He also went to school out there," Ann said, "when it was 'The Annex.'"

I told her I knew The Annex well.

"Actually, I've met several other men who also lived out there during their first year of college at A&M." I pointed to Billy Lay across the room.

The “fish” of Barracks 306, including Ann Burns’ future husband, Curtis (*fifth from right on front row*). Courtesy of Ann Burns.

"Our son took classes out there, too, after the university took control," Ann added.

With others waiting to say hello and not wanting to monopolize my time, Ann thanked me for my talk and excused herself. As she was leaving, I spoke up.

"Would you be willing to let me interview you for the 'RELLIS Recollections' project?" I asked.

"Of course!" she replied as she made her way out of the room.

Nearly four months later, Ann finally sat in front of my camera. We shot the interview in a training room at the TEEX headquarters building located in the College Station Business Center. Arlen Crouch had driven Ann to the location, and she was under the impression we were on the RELLIS Campus.

I did not correct her.

After exchanging pleasantries to put her at ease, I asked her to tell me her "RELLIS story."

"As a young girl growing up in Bryan, I remember my parents taking me out to where the Air Force base would be built. It was called 'Riverside' back then, and we would buy fresh vegetables and strawberries from the farmers there.

"My father worked for the local gas company, and he helped put in the gas lines during construction of Bryan Field. He took me out there a time or two. It was all very exciting.

"I was probably about 10 years old at the time."

By no means did Ann's RELLIS recollections end there.

"Curtis and I were classmates in high school, and we started going together then. In 1948, he came out here as a freshman. Of course, women weren't admitted to A&M at the time, so I went off to TSCW (Texas State College for Women, now Texas Women's University).

"I have pictures of 'Barracks 306.' Curtis lived there as a freshman and he had many stories about the things that happened at the old Annex."

At that point, Ann merely raised her eyebrows and smiled, which elicited an off-camera chuckle from her interviewer.

I knew well of the high jinx and pranks marooned teenagers came up with at The Annex when they became bored.

Curtis Burns enrolled in college shortly after the Air Force became an independent branch of the service. After his graduation from A&M, he accepted a commission to become an Air Force officer, intending to become a fighter pilot.

Curtis and Ann were married in 1952. After basic training and flight school, Curtis was assigned to Bryan Air Force Base in 1954 to train as a fighter-pilot.

Ultimately, Curtis Burns rose to the rank of major and retired from the Air Force in 1973. He and Ann again returned to Bryan, in part because their son, Glen, was having troubles in high school.

"Glen suffered from dyslexia and had a hard time with his classwork," Ann said. "But he was gifted with his hands.

"After we came back, Curtis took a job as an administrator in the Mays School of Business at the college. He found Glen an electronics course at the old air base, and Glen came out to take classes there.

Ann's story suddenly took an unexpected turn.

"The program was called the Institute of Electronic Design, and Glen was doing very well. He was about six weeks from graduating when he left class for the day out there. As always, he drove past the main gate, which was on Highway 21, and turned right to come home.

"He got about a quarter of a mile down the road when a car veered into his lane, hit him, and killed him instantly."

Glen Burns was 20 when he died the afternoon of May 19, 1976.

Curtis Burns passed away in early 2012. In retirement, he and Ann returned to the old Bryan Air Force Base site to help with a TTI research project.

"We volunteered to read the new road signs they were developing at the time," Ann said. "They were testing various fonts and colors. We would drive 60 miles an hour down the runway at night and push a button when we could read the signs.

"We got $15 a night for the work!"

Unknown to Arlen Crouch, Fremont Burger took his Astro-Kinetic

Glen Burns (*middle row, third from left*) and his fellow classmates of the Texas Engineering Extension Service Institute of Electronic Science class. Courses were held at the Research Annex. Courtesy of Ann Burns.

The Astro-Kinetic Lift was briefly located at the Texas A&M Research Annex in 1963. The "flying-saucer" shaped machine was created to be a vertical-lift aircraft. Courtesy of *Popular Science* magazine.

Lift and left the Research Annex for the San Antonio Municipal Airport where he continued his efforts to give his bird flight.

There, his company teamed with Howard Aero Services, and on December 16, 1964, a dramatically redesigned craft—which resembled a white steampunk hat more than a flying saucer—successfully took flight, but rose only a few feet off the ground and for only a short amount of time.

Burger did not win the Navy contract. He died at his Houston home shortly after receiving the news.

After interviewing Crouch, I dug deeper into the Dyna-Lift story, eventually learning of its bitter end. Crouch had been unaware of what had happened to Burger or his proposed invention.

Ironically, the Coandă affect is presently employed in a series of aircraft built by MD Helicopters, a former subsidiary of McDonnell Douglas. A "NOTAR" system—standing for "no tail rotor"—employs the same principle as the Dyna-Lift, but only inside the tail boom.

Fremont Burger had been ahead of his time.

Meeting both Crouch and Burns, as well as the dozens of others who graciously allowed me to capture their recollections of the 75-year history of today's RELLIS Campus, has been a gratifying experience. A complete list of the interviewees featured on the RELLIS website is contained at the end of this book.

The stories here are but a small sampling of the impact the old Bryan Army Air Field and its later iterations have had on the local community, the state, and, in many respects, the nation as well.

Consider that Bryan Field wasn't intended to become a permanent fixture. In large part, it was built—save for its runways—to be disassembled. On December 7, 1941, the US Army Air Forces had 114 airfields in the continental United States. Two years later, that number swelled to 783.

So temporary were many of the structures at Bryan Field that some were moved into the city. At least one old barracks, split into two and refurbished, still serves today as a comfortable and attractive home for a local retired couple.

Many World War II–era bases remain active, like Vance Air Force Base in my hometown of Enid, Oklahoma. Others were converted to civilian use, like Austin-Bergstrom Airport.

Chief among its lasting tributes, today's RELLIS Campus has always been a place for dreamers, as you've read here:

T. O. Walton, Joseph Duckworth, Travis B. Bryan, Elwood Driver, Joan Michaels, Suzanne Delano, Buzz Aldrin, Gus Grissom, John Porter, Billy Lay, Regina Stetz, Tony Cordasco, Dionysius Roxs, Russell Hillier, Earl Rudder, Dick Zimmer, Lamar and Kyle McNew, Glen Burns, Dick Steffy, Bob Rudder, Lilia Gonzalez, Juliana Rangel, Kathy Banks, Gary Sera, and John Sharp.

Countless lives have been transformed where RELLIS stands today. Innumerable discoveries have been made there. And although much of what once was is now gone, enough remains—in the old chapel, control tower, flight-line hangars, and runways—that the past has been adequately preserved.

What matters now is that the future of RELLIS is equally compelling to its past. New activities and accomplishments are generated there each and every day.

Some, again, may change the world.

And all are worthy of their own place in tomorrow's accounts of history in the making.

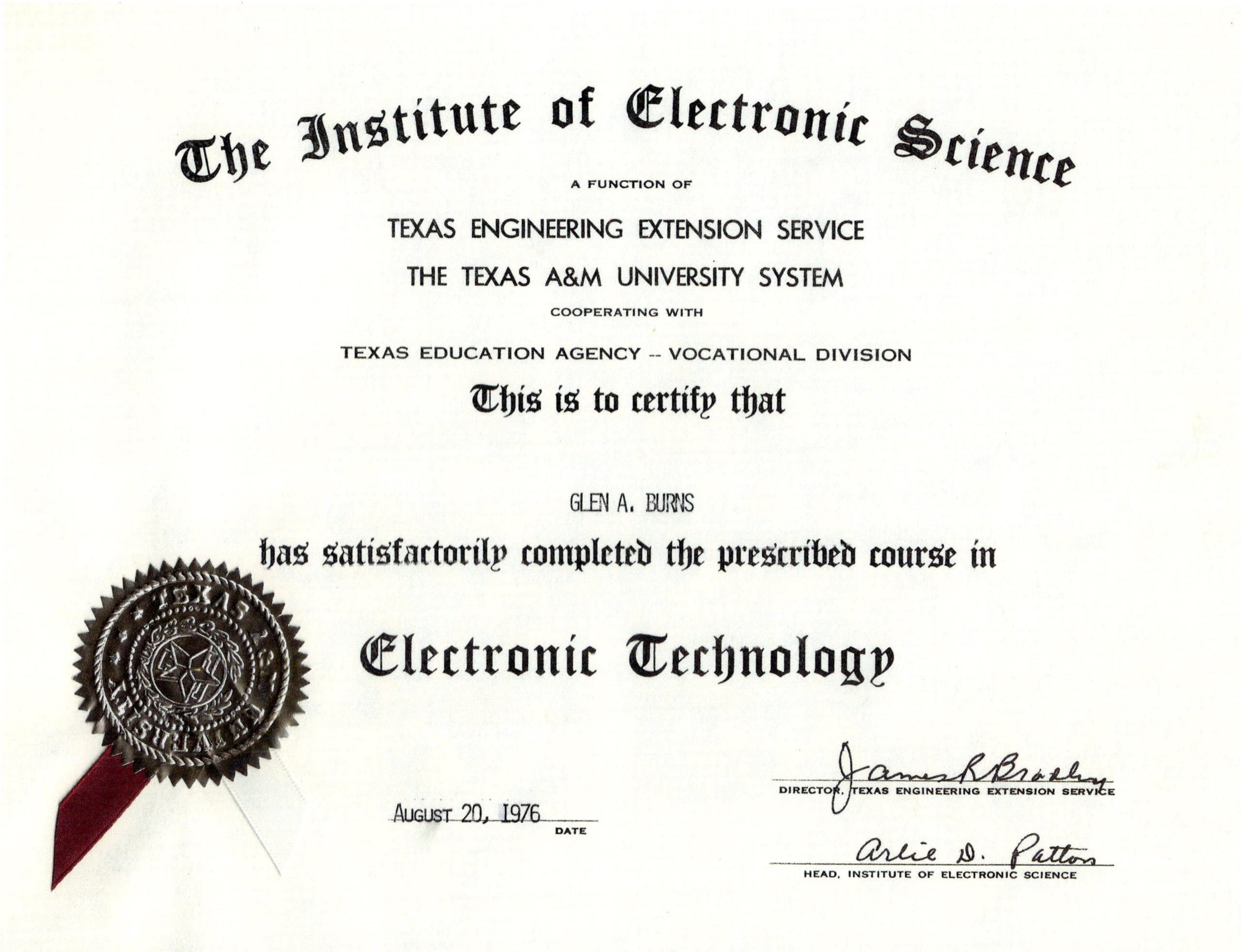
The Institute of Electronic Science

A FUNCTION OF

TEXAS ENGINEERING EXTENSION SERVICE

THE TEXAS A&M UNIVERSITY SYSTEM

COOPERATING WITH

TEXAS EDUCATION AGENCY -- VOCATIONAL DIVISION

This is to certify that

GLEN A. BURNS

has satisfactorily completed the prescribed course in

Electronic Technology

AUGUST 20, 1976
DATE

DIRECTOR, TEXAS ENGINEERING EXTENSION SERVICE

HEAD, INSTITUTE OF ELECTRONIC SCIENCE

Burns' IES certificate, awarded posthumously. Courtesy of Ann Burns.

ORAL HISTORY CONTRIBUTORS

John A. Adams
Phil Adams
Buzz Aldrin
Dennis Allen
Jay Anderson
Greg Bailey
Kathy Banks
John Barton
Gene Barber
Kem Bennett
Matthew Bizzell
Roger Bligh
Larry Boleman
Robert Borden
Anne Boykin
Blanche Brick
Bob Brick
Gary Briers
James Bright
Tim Bryan
Karen Buck
Lance Bullard
Ann Burns
Gene Buth
Bob Byrns
David Chapman
David Claridge
Jerry Cooper
Tony Cordasco
Arlen Crouch
Lee Denham
Harry Elemendorf
Gordon Evans
Kathy Fraser
Dale Fritz
Zachary Grasley
Mark Grissom
Rosalba Gutierrez
Donny Hamilton
Arnold Hayes
Mary Hensley
Jim Keblinger
Chris Kirk
Bill Lay
James Loya
Henry Mayo
Chris Marrs
Jett McFalls
B. F. McLemore
Kyle McNew
Lamar McNew
Wanda Menges
Jack Millender
Wally Moon
Ellis Mooring
Andrew Nelson
John Nielsen-Gammon
Charles & Regina Opersteny
Mary Jo Prince
Juliana Rangel
Mian N. Riaz
Gerald Ryan
Wayne Sadberry
Charles M. "Red" Scott
Gary Sera
John Sharp
Loren Steffy
Kelly Templin
Tom Turbiville
Jorge Vanegas
DaNeetra Walker
Joe West
Joe Williams
Gregory Winfree
David Woodcock
Bill Youngkin
Donna Zatopek
Dick Zimmer

ACKNOWLEDGMENTS

The vision for this book and its companion website stems directly from the imagination of the individual who conceived the idea of the RELLIS Campus, Texas A&M University System Chancellor John Sharp.

Few figures in recent Texas history stand taller than the chancellor. As a longtime admirer of both his work and public demeanor, I have considered it a privilege assembling these stories and I hope this work measures up to his expectations.

There are many others to thank in this RELLIS journey of mine.

I came to Aggieland as a trailing spouse. My wife, Nancy Currie-Gregg, accepted a position as professor in the Texas A&M College of Engineering's Industrial & Systems Engineering Department. Thus, we and our three dogs resettled from Houston to the Brazos Valley.

My first local was Mark Klemm, assistant vice president for development at the Texas A&M University Foundation. Mark and his family have known Nancy for many years through a church connection. Mark is the embodiment of what "RELLIS" stands for: respect, excellence, leadership, loyalty, integrity, and selfless service.

Through Mark I met Kathryn Greenwade, the vice president for human resources at the Association of Former Students of Texas A&M. Kathryn graciously passed my name around campus, which is how I became acquainted with Laylan Copelin.

I've long been a fan of Laylan's work as an investigative reporter for the Austin American-Statesman. Now the vice chancellor of marketing and communications for the A&M system, just meeting Laylan for lunch was a treat. He not only introduced me to one of the best taco diners in town, but also handed me the reins to pull together RELLIS Recollections.

That story has now been told, in large part, through the experience and remembrances of those listed on the Oral History Contributors pages of this book. To each and every one who welcomed me and my video cameras into their lives, I offer a humble "thank you." Without your involvement, RELLIS history would be slowly vanishing today.

A special thank you to two people on that contributor's roster. Greg Bailey is the curator of the Cushing Library and chief archivist for the university. On multiple occasions, he and his staff brought boxes from storage for me to peruse in the Cushing Reading Room in my search for understanding this work. Greg is a marvel, his vast knowledge is a valuable asset to Texas A&M and its historical legacy.

Special thanks, too, to David Woodcock, professor emeritus in the Texas A&M College of Architecture and founder of the university's Center for Heritage Conservation. Thanks to his previous work at the Riverside Campus, I began to develop a clearer and more complete picture of what the center had once been and what it was to become anew.

Perhaps my biggest debt of gratitude goes to Bill Page of the Texas A&M University Libraries. He, too, is an asset-extraordinaire to his alma mater. From seemingly out of nowhere, Bill stepped into my work and through a multitude of emails, he opened doors to RELLIS's past that I would never have been able to find. Much of what you read here about the Tuskegee Airmen and the WASPs who served at Bryan Army Air Field came from sources Bill found. I thank him for his generous support and investment of time. He truly possesses a genuine fascination and affection for Texas A&M's proud past.

To the editors, past and present of The Eagle newspaper in Bryan, I say thanks to Kelly Brown for setting me on the right track and to Darren Benson for graciously previewing many of the stories found within the pages this book.

To the staff at Texas A&M University Press, thank you for shepherding this book home.

To the readers, I hope this book brings back memories and instills in you a desire to contribute to the ongoing excavation of the RELLIS Campus story, what for decades was a bit of a mystery on the banks of the Brazos River.

And finally, to my wife. Your own story constantly inspired my telling of the RELLIS narrative. As in days gone by at RELLIS, you too, served your country as an army aviator. Like Bryan Air Force Base pilots Buzz Aldrin and Gus Grissom, you flew fearlessly into space. You have devoted yourself to the education of tomorrow's visionaries and to the pursuit of applied knowledge which will make the world better place.

Almost every day I spent at RELLIS, I found something there that reminded me of you.

Index

NOTE: Page numbers in *italic* type indicate information contained in images or image captions